THE RECALIBRATION OF HUMANITY

2013 and Beyond

Kryon
Book 13

RECALIBRATION

(1) To correct a measuring process by checking or adjusting again in comparison with a standard.

(2) To make corrections in, or adjust a procedure or process.

(Metaphysics)
To recognize the standard of "the way things were," and readjust the reality of life by recalibration that reality to "the way things can be." To change the standard by which all things are measured, spiritually. To readjust "normal."

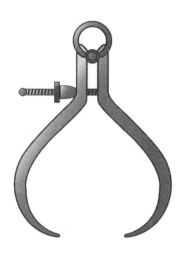

In memory of...

Sid Wolf

A Kryon team member for many years; my healer and
mentor, and my friend. Sid, thank you for showing me
how the body works, and what is possible that I only
once dreamed of. Thank you for being such an amazing
part of the Kryon team for well over a decade. I will see
you again the next time around.
The love connection remains...

In memory of...

Steve Jobs

We never knew each other, but every Kryon book for
twenty three years has been produced on a Macintosh.
Every flyer, post card, and website has been designed
on a Mac. Every photo of every seminar has been
enhanced and presented... on a Mac. All my communications are done on an iphone, and the ipad rocks! You
profoundly affected every Kryon fan with this
technology, and never knew it.

I'll miss *"just one more thing..."*

THE RECALIBRATION OF HUMANITY
2013 and Beyond
Kryon Book 13

Publisher: The Kryon Writings, Inc.

P.O. Box 28871
San Diego
California 92198

Kryon books can be purchased in retail stores,
by phone or on the Internet at [www.kryon.com/store].
(800) 352-6657 - E-mail <kryonbooks@kryon.com>

Written by Lee Carroll, Ph.D (hon)
Cover Design by DeLisiArt
Primary Editing by Dawne Brooks
Secondary Editing by Lois M. Grant, Ph.D.
Copyright © 2013—The Kryon Writings, Inc.
Printed in the United States of America
First Printing—November 2013
Second Printing—February 2014
Third Printing—October 2014

ISBN# 1-888053-22-4 $16.98

Table of Contents

INTRODUCTION
Lee Carroll 7

CHAPTER ONE
The Recalibration of The Human Being........................... 39
   Kryon

CHAPTER TWO
The Recalibration of Knowlege 55
   Kryon

CHAPTER THREE
The Channelling Experience 75
   Lee Carroll

CHAPTER FOUR
The Recalibration of The Universe 81
   Kryon

CHAPTER FIVE
The Recalibration of Dark and Light................................ 93
   Kryon

CHAPTER SIX
The Recalibration of "Shoulds" 111
   Kryon

CHAPTER SEVEN
The Recalibration of Free Choice.................................... 123
   Kryon

CHAPTER EIGHT
The Recalibration of Gaia 139
   Kryon

CHAPTER NINE
The Recalibration of Self - Part One 153
   Kryon

Table of Contents - continued...

CHAPTER TEN
The Recalibration of Self - Part Two.. 167
    Kryon

CHAPTER ELEVEN
The Recalibration of Self - Part Three 185
    Kryon

CHAPTER TWELVE
The Recalibration of the Crystalline Grid 199
    Kryon

CHAPTER THIRTEEN
The Elusive Akash 211
    Kryon

CHAPTER FOURTEEN
The Three Winds 229
    Kryon

FINAL THOUGHTS
    Lee Carroll.. 252

KRYON INFORMATION 254

INDEX 262

Introduction

Lee Carroll

Kryon
Book 13

Introduction
Kryon Book 13
by Lee Carroll

Greetings and welcome to Kryon Book 13. I am Lee Carroll, original channel for Kryon, and as I write this, it is my 24th year representing Kryon, a grand angelic energy.

This is the place in my books where I normally explain Kryon and also tell you some personal experiences that have occurred since the last book. This is also where I discuss how seemingly strange and odd channelling appears to the minds of those who might be reading a Kryon book for the first time.

However, after all this time I'm still an engineer at heart, a hermit in my reality, and feel very much like a normal guy (some of my family would disagree). But I'm also very aware of how all this looks to the average person who was taught in their church that perhaps what I do is evil (ho hum). Hey, this is also Book 13, so it has to be spooky, huh? If you think any of that, then just put the book away. It's not for you.

I'm realizing that the "Kryon community" has grown greatly in the past few years and that Kryonites (not a substance that hurts Superman) are the people who have picked up this book – weird people like me. So I'm compelled to skip all the things I used to say at this point in my opening remarks to explain the weirdness and, instead, just reference my past books for these explanations. There are far more amazing pieces of information to give you about the revelation of the timing of our planet, the energies that are being felt, and the incredible changes before us.

"What? Lee, you are not going to tell us more about some of the odd things that have happened to you in the years of travelling to exotic

places around the planet?" OK, perhaps I will, but only in reference to the subjects that I cover as the story unfolds about what is really happening to Earth.

The Veiled Prophecy

I was born in California in the United States and spent the first 40 or so years of my life without being interested in any esoteric, New Age, or indigenous information. Like most of the population, I was immersed in my culture and only paid attention to religious attributes to the extent I was interested. But it wouldn't have mattered if I was a Christian or Jewish, since we all got information about the future from Holy Scripture of some kind. Even if you were a once-a-year church or synagogue attendee, you still were exposed to a basic idiom: The prophecies of the planet were about what was going to happen to us at the millennium and how the end times would play out.

Early on, I can remember evangelists coming to our town and telling us about how the Middle East was going to set the stage for everything – all the horror. There was talk of rapture and books about being "left behind". There were more books from biblical scholars and an all-around agreement that something big was going to happen when we got to 2000 – big and bad (or good, if you were one of the chosen). The scary part was that over the years, things in the news were seemingly validating all this prophecy.

The Middle East was right on track with the evangelists' scenarios (scary). Then there was Nostradamus, a pseudo-astrologer who channelled the future, but who wrote in mysterious quatrains to keep his associates from knowing what he was into. His writings, interpreted carefully by scholars over the years, pretty much were in line with the evangelists' preachings! Now, that was really scary! I grew up with this.

We all heard these doom predictions back then, even before The History Channel decided to make its life's work about scaring people for commercial reasons. (The "history" name is just a ruse to get you to think they are experts about the future. They are not. The only thing they do well is, ah, *history!*) The prevailing doom and gloom information was also in bookstores everywhere, occasionally on TV, and in more recent years, on the Internet.

So this was our modern-day prophecy, and most of those who would read my words here were exposed to it, and there wasn't much else to counter what might have really been going on (the subject of this book). In fact, even in the New Age, many were hopping on the "doom bus"!

In the '80s, a famous channeller in Yelm, Washington, told people to prepare for the coming millennium by building underground shelters in their homes (at great cost). They were to have air filtration systems (for the radiation) and storehouses for at least a year of canned food. They were told to create the safe chamber below their homes at least 2 meters (6 feet) underground so they wouldn't get zapped by radiation. You might roll your eyes and ask, "Who would build this?" The answer is that many did! Today in Yelm, there are still real estate offerings that specify if the property has a "UG" (underground). Check it out. (In some cases, a UG cost up to $200,000 to build.) Fear costs quite a bit.

Another famous New Age author was telling her followers to head for the hills (many did), and yet still another was stating that the earth was going to flip upside down! The advice on how to escape this "flip" always amused me, since there simply is no escape from a physical polar flip. We all go flying off into space along with the oceans and the air, but science normally isn't really considered in these kinds of fear-based messages. But it was all centered around the coming doom energy of the millennium, the year 2000.

Zecharia Sitchin was kind of a self-made historian of the Sumerian culture, which he dated at about 10,000 years ago. He was one of the few back in the '80s who could actually read Sumerian. His information centered on a mysterious planet called Nibiru (The Twelfth Planet). Some said it was going to zip into our solar system from an elongated elliptical orbit and collide with us in 2003. It didn't (as I recall), and so when it didn't happen, the prophecy was updated by others to be 2012. It didn't happen then either (as I recall). CNN actually covered his prophecy on the solstice on December 21, 2012! (They didn't think it would happen either.) Sitchin left us in 2010, but was instrumental in influencing some mainstream science fiction films, including the 2011 release of the movie *Cowboys and Aliens*, which featured a Sitchin premise of gold-mining aliens.

Look at the similarities here. It didn't matter what spiritual system you were part of, each had its doom message and it was all centered around the years leading up to, and out of, the millennium. Overwhelmingly, the information was generally the same – we simply were not going to make it. That theme was everywhere and seemingly came from almost all spiritual sources. Hollywood, of course, just couldn't keep still, and two years before the end of the Mayan calendar's long count, they produced a disaster movie called *2012*. It was a comedy (as I saw it).

So here I sit at the end of 2013 (as I write this 13th book), and we didn't perish (as I also recall). I keep saying that because I'm constantly being told that as a senior, I'm approaching a time when I won't recall much.

The Constant Bias – It Won't Go Away

We are now firmly past the 2012 marker, but the old prophecies just won't die. The great rapture novel series entitled "Left Behind" has now been made into a movie, even though the rapture date has long gone. "Survivalists" is a TV series about people who are getting ready for the end. Nobody told them that the end didn't happen, I guess. The truth about all this is that it takes about 6 or 7 years to sell movies and TV series, so they finally sold these ideas and went ahead anyway, even after "doomsday" passed. Fear sells no matter what the facts are, so even though all the doom dates are past and the scriptural rapture dates have come and gone several times, the cash machine continues to ring for those who just love to watch things that scare them, even though they don't make much sense. Welcome to Hollywood.

I think my favorite rapture book of the last 10 years was one written in response to the Christian doom books. The "Left Behind" books were a series of exciting novels about those who were left behind after the rapture. They were co-written by a fundamentalist Baptist minister in my city named Tim Lahaye. I met him a couple of times when I was a young boy (nice guy). But the book I just love is *I Want To Be Left Behind!* by Ted Noel, another Christian minister who was pointing out the fallacy of Tim's tweaking of the scripture to make his books better sellers and action-packed enough for a movie. What? You mean there was dissension of opinion between Christians? Yes. Amazing.

So it's not going away. There is an entire generation of humanity who still believes the end is coming, just like it was coming when I was a kid. We were constantly afraid we wouldn't be ready and, even to this day, I continue to hear this message from the church in general. So I guess "the end is always coming", and in certain circles people will live their lives fearing what has been proven over and over to be a fallacy. The dates of our doom will continue to be updated, and people will scamper to keep pace with the doom information. They are glued to those who tell them all about a very loving God who is going to kill them horribly by fire if they don't do what they are told by those who are the "appointed authorities of God", often in funny hats and costumes. (Hey, at least I don't wear a funny costume when I channel.)

I stood on a stage in Moscow in May 2012 on the very date when a famous evangelist named Harold Camping had announced that the world would end. Even in Moscow they had heard about it, but (as I recall) nothing happened. Although it didn't happen, he updated the doom date to October 21. I guess he didn't have enough egg on his face from the first misfire. Naturally, again, nothing happened. More egg, but no accountability.

This kind of thing will continue and continue until a full generation of people knows better. Even then, there will be the holdouts from other cultures that depend on this information to feel guilty for living and have a need to suffer or worry to somehow feel spiritual. I have yet to understand why people who have been delivered from dictators and authoritative governments fully expect to be eventually returned to that state. As I travel the world, it's interesting to see some cultures who "know better" and others who are ready to believe almost anything from anyone.

Cooking Under the Hood

What if I told you that there has been another prophecy known all over the earth by many who don't even know each other, and that this information pre-dated any prophecy that you grew up with? It is thousands of years old, much older than Christianity or most of the scriptures on the planet. Interested? I was!

This prophecy is real and will be the subject of this book. This is information that was "always there" but that didn't have the impact of the modern-day doom and gloom. It wasn't as glamorous, for it told of positive potentials of great shift and balance. The wild thing is that almost all the indigenous peoples of the planet knew it all along. But then, they don't make the movies.

Gregg Braden is a friend of mine and one of the finest speakers and lecturers around today. He is a scientist (with credentials) and spent the first part of his career helping to design rockets. Later, he helped manage large technical groups with Cisco Systems. I tell you this just to let you know his background. When Gregg began studying the Ancients, his mindset changed, and his academic endeavors led him right into what we are looking at today. There is another great truth out there, and the Ancients had been talking about it for thousands of years.

Gregg brings some of these ancient writings into his lectures. He personally leads tours to Tibet and Peru (areas of the earth that are playing a great part in the energy shift), and he is an author writing on the science and history that he has discovered along the way. In his lectures and books, he has stated that his research in these areas has led him to a conclusion. It appears that we have had a number of "decision points" along the way in Human history where we may have completely lost cultures and all information to that point. Civilization may have even *started over* a number of times. In addition, Gregg tells us that humanity has a tendency to develop consciousness in waves over time, which appears to be something that can be calculated and predicted.

Fractal Time (2009) is one of Gregg's many books, and in it, he reports his findings from a scientific point of view. Using the Ancients' information, he applies these new "laws" of fractals to "ancient waves of time". He proposes that everything from the way we age to our patterns of relationships and even wars between nations are simply the returning waves of our past. As each wave returns, it carries a more amplified version of itself. Say what? Is it possible there is a system of time and consciousness that is a cycle? Does this really exist? Is this new?

Enter the Maya

In Kryon Book 11, I tell of my brief time at Xochicalco, a smallish ancient Mayan archeological dig outside of Mexico City. In 2007 I met an engineer who was recreating the circumstances that allowed the Maya to view the heavens and produce their famous calendars. Using their own underground observatories at that very place, Jorge Baez was spending hundreds of hours in the dark. The only light in the cavern was a small amount from the sun and moon, which shone down a long vertical tunnel from the surface. By directing it through a series of small holes that the Maya had designed along the shaft, the light eventually formed a focused image on a table placed on the dirt floor where it could be analyzed. With his engineering background, Jorge was searching for what the Maya could actually see back then and how they might have interpreted it. The curators of Xochicalco had actually given Jorge the key to the place!

Jorge wrote a book (Spanish language only at this time) called *The Secret of 2012, The Vital Energy of Movement.* This was the story of his work, spending time in these Mayan ruins and actually seeing what the Maya saw back then. As small a measurement as it is, he indicated that using their methods, he was even able to see the wobble of the earth, much as they did. This wobble is known in astronomy as the Precession of the Equinoxes, and it relates to (ready?) fractal time. The Mayan calendar may have actually been the template for exactly what Gregg had been talking about.

By the way, just for fun and as a review, I again mention that this is the place where we did the orb experiment that I published in Kryon Book 11. You can still see it on my website at www.kryon. com/orbs. Can someone actually create orbs? What are they? This webpage only answers the first question. Imagine creating orbs in this underground Mayan observatory! We did it, and I again invite you to take a look at some very fun photos!

Jorge eventually took me from the depths of the Mayan underground observatory out into the sun for more lessons. He carefully showed and explained the glyphs on the walls of a smallish Mayan pyramid. The writing was pristine and very readable (if you read Mayan). It was their explanation of fractal time and represented a repeating pattern of potential Human consciousness. (This pattern often was presented in waves of time called *pachacuti* – a timeline with segments of 500 years each.) Each pachacuti had an approximate 30-year beginning and end and was a time of immense change for humanity. We are exactly in that now!

The pattern was obvious when you looked at the glyphs with Jorge's eyes and experience. The striations etched into the pyramid walls indicated the potentials in a timeline of the future where humanity might have cycles of both high and low consciousness as predicted by this system. The Mayan symbols and glyphs physically swept up and down in a very graphic way, showing the same pattern of predictions that they report in their calendar. I took a photo of this and, to this day, it's one of my favorites that I showed for years in my seminars. It wasn't hidden or mysterious or in need of massive scholarly interpretation. Anyone who could read Mayan could see what they had predicted. By the way, there are lots of Mayans remaining, and they know how to read the ancient writing, so I always tell people, "If you don't believe me, just ask a Mayan!"

This information of consciousness potential relating to time is not an obvious connection to our future unless you are standing there putting all this together with an archeologist at your side. Is it possible that the Maya had discovered this cycle of potential, the same one Gregg had written about? If so, then why all the doom and gloom from the mass media? And why does The History Channel (and others) tell you that the Mayan calendar ended in 2012?

The answer is complex, but the truth is that the Maya had many priests, and these men were not necessarily the calendar makers. Like any culture, there were complexities in personalities, politics, and power structure. For us to think they were all simple-minded people who just had one idea and followed one tribal king's doctrines through their entire history is very naive. Yet many have portrayed them this way in movies (Thanks, Mel). The truth is that their leadership was constantly in turmoil, much like the Egyptians and the Romans. Both of these latter cultures had absolute leaders with absolute power, too, but if you study history, you learn there were disagreements and covert schemes and power shifts all the time. Assassinations were common and there was a constant struggle to be "in favor with the guy on the throne", or to actually *be* the guy on the throne, or to keep from being killed by the guy on the throne.

So even in their spiritual priesthoods, there was competition. Imagine that! They argued about spiritual things? Scandalous! Therefore, our Mayan information today is a meld of all these ideas and personalities, both calendar and non-calendar related. The most famous of these are the *Chilam Balam* prophecies, or so-called *Jaguar Priest* prophecies. They are dark and were developed outside of the calendar work, mostly on the Yucatan Peninsula. There were actually many Maya prophecies about the end of the world, depending on which priest you listened to. So, who was right?

If you have visited the Mayan Riviera, or perhaps been in any Mayan ruin, there is often a ball court represented. This court was used for many ceremonies, and some of them were gruesome. They often brought conquered kings and priests from other regions and beheaded them here in a victory celebration. They played games to see who would live and die. So it was in that tradition where the question of which priest had the right "message from Spirit" got settled. It was decided by a now famous team-based game, which the individual Mayan settlements played with a small ball and hoop.

Using only their heads and feet, knees and elbows, the first team to get the ball through the hoop won. The priest who represented that team then got the validation of his spiritual information and won for that day. So they used the game to let "chance" or "fate" settle the dispute, just as they did for who would live or die in their victory celebrations. But they did it often! That should tell you how much variation there was in competing spiritual information.

The game was serious (life and death) and only one goal (ball through the hoop) won the game. It ended with a ceremony of the losing captain being killed. I suppose the death was an honor for him (like much of their Human sacrifice was supposed to be), but I really wonder if that guy felt that way at the moment of the loss when the other team's ball went through the hoop.

So all the hoop-la (pun intended) regarding the Mayan calendar information leading up to 2012 was due in part to all this complexity. It wasn't pure calendar information at all, and it got mixed in a great deal with the games they played and information garnered from priests who had their own agendas (and had won some games).

By the way, you can see a watered down recreation of this game (without the death at the end) at Xcaret in Cancun, Mexico, where tourists go to play and have fun. If you go to almost any Mayan ruins, you can also see what is left of the actual stadiums where they played the games. I've seen them mostly in Mexico at Coba, Xochicalco, and Chichen Itza.

The Maya calendar guys just kept doing their calendar, however, and the thing that was amazing in all this was that the winter solstice of 2012 turns out to be a fractal time decision point. It was also the year of the Galactic Alignment, the start and stop point of the 26,000-year precession of the equinoxes (remember from above?). This alignment is caused by a 26,000-year wobble of the planet that starts and ends when our sun perfectly lines up (as we look at it from earth) with the center of our galaxy (as close as we can discern this).

So the solstice of December 21, 2012, represents a fractal time point, along with some other priests' ideas, too. It also represented doom in our culture, due to The History Channel's profound ability to decide what personalities to put on television that can portray the most believable and convincing fear of things that don't exist and never will happen.

By the way, is anyone out there ever going to write a letter to these guys and hold them accountable for scaring our kids? How many years of horror predictions that just don't happen does it take for us to object to the programming?

The Galactic Alignment

I don't want to give a bigger discourse on this 2012 alignment than is needed, since it's easily found on the 'net. Look for it within *astronomy*, not *New Age*, and don't use Wikipedia please. It's a very biased pseudo-information service that is often wrong; educators won't use it and we shouldn't either.

The wobble of the earth affects how we see the sky, and most of the Ancients we study somehow knew about it and recorded it for us to see that they knew it. Say what? Ancients knew about the wobble of the earth? Yep.

At this point, I love to point something out that very few think about. How did the Ancients know about galactic motion, yet only a few hundred years ago we didn't know the earth was round?! Does it look like we might have lost some knowledge along the way? I think Gregg Braden is right on with his research and we may have lost a great deal of good science and observation through waves of time in our past. The *decision points* he speaks of may, indeed, have happened. Common sense starts to come in handy when we see that the Ancients knew about our place in the galaxy, yet those who sailed from Europe only a few centuries ago were afraid they would fall of the edge of the earth.

I also find it interesting to look at some other TV series that are finding popularity. There are now historians from universities actually asking the question if there was a whole civilization before "known civilization". Could it be that the American continent was well known by the Europeans hundreds of years before Columbus? It might be so, according to some overwhelming evidence that is starting to show itself.

Europeans may have actually traded with those on the American continent for things as advanced as mined copper! This is startling information, since it not only rewrites history, but may give a hint that we somehow lost centuries of information that we have no idea about. It's buried deep, indicating that it was long, long ago.

It's really interesting to look at a few things that play into the 2012 energy. First, I want you to understand a little astronomy. You don't have to ponder this much, just read about it here. Our galaxy is a spiral galaxy, and if you have seen photos of other spiral galaxies (like Andromeda), most of the billions of stars are clumped together in a big narrow ring around the middle (like a dish). So as we look at the sky on a dark night, that "ring" is the stripe in the sky, and we call it the *Milky Way*. Our solar system is in that galactic ring, of course, so it makes sense that our Galactic Alignment of 2012 would be right in the middle of it, as we see it in the sky.

As the wobble of the earth approaches the place where the start and finish of the wobble are measured, it "precesses through the Milky Way". (I told you not to ponder it much.) That just means that when the sun lines up exactly with the center of our galaxy as we observe it from Earth, it is positioned right in the middle of that Milky Way stripe in the sky. So the alignment has us looking through that galactic ring, right into the center of our galaxy.

Astronomers often call this ring edge of our galaxy, "The Dark Rift." This is because in a telescope, you can see many huge, dark gas clouds in space obscuring other stars. We can't really see these dark places well with the naked eye, unless there is no light at all around us at night as we view the sky. Then it shows. These dark places in the Milky Way are really obvious when you know where to look. It's so obvious that the Ancients had names for the dark places, just like they had names for the constellations.

The Timing of the Alignment

As this very slow alignment takes place, it "walks us" into the Milky Way stripe in the sky, and it takes 36 years (or approximately three decades) to get through the whole thing. It takes 18 years to "precess" to the middle of the stripe and 18 years to get out of it. So there are 18 years on each side of the actual Galactic Alignment. The center alignment was the solstice of 2012, and then our planet continues to wobble into another 26,000-year cycle. This 36-year period is also an energy alignment. The indigenous as well as esoteric prophets have told us that this alignment is when a potential SHIFT will happen.

Let's stop for a moment. Did you ever hear any prophecies about the end of 2012 creating, "three days of darkness"? Many did, and we didn't get it (as I recall). Or did we? There is so much prophecy that is written as metaphors. Most of Nostradamus' work is written that way, and a great deal of the verses in the Book of Revelation in the Holy Bible are, too. What if the prophecies of "three days of darkness" have actually happened? Stay with me here.

As mentioned above, the precession takes a little over 30 years as it slowly moves through (ready?) *The Dark Rift* (the astronomy name given to it). So what if the whole idea of the three days of darkness was the description of the very thing we are experiencing right now – three decades of moving through The Dark Rift? I like that, since it explains why such a scary prophecy didn't happen the way some expected.

When I realized the timing of all this, I looked around at my own work, and I also looked at those who I work with – channellers, authors, readers, and healers. Almost without exception, their path of realized enlightenment had taken place within the past 18 to 22 years. This was the beginning of the transition through the 36-year window of the final phase of the wobble – the great shift.

I also looked at the signs of when it all started. The 11:11 – Harmonic Convergence of 1987 was a precursor to this shift, almost announcing it! By 1994 (the beginning of the 18 years), I had produced the first two Kryon books. It was all starting to fit the ancient predictions and supported the fractal time idea.

The Soviet Union also fell over right before the beginning of the alignment and changed all the prophecy of the "modern doom" we had been told about. Did you ever wonder how such a dramatic event as the fall of the Soviets was never on Nostradamus' schedule? It wasn't in the Holy Bible's Book of Revelation, either. It was a surprise to everyone (especially our own Pentagon). Could it be that the very paradigm of our Human civilization was about to change? Could it be that we had decided not to end it all again, but this time to go right through the alignment into a new energy?

Back to the Calendar

The Mayan calendar we grew up with is finished. It ended in 2012. Quite simply, it was the end of the Mayan "long count". It's complicated, but pretend it's like the calendar you have on the wall. At the end of the year (our count is 365 days), it ends. Then what happens? We put another calendar on the wall, a new one. That's what the Maya do, only less often, and they have calendars on the shelf in "calendar language" out to the year 4000. So it was never the "end of time". It was simply the end of their current calendar. But you know that personally, right? You are still here and it's 2013 (just doing a reality check). By the way, just ask a Mayan about this. They will breathe a sigh of relief now that all this fear business assigned to them is over.

But the Maya knew the significance of the end of this cycle, for it represented something so final that they needed a new calendar and a new count. I remember what Jorge Baez showed me on the stone glyphs. There was a giant sweep up (representing Human potential) and the interpretation around it was, "the potential for the highest consciousness that humanity had ever seen" – 2013.

I like the work of another academic, Geoff Stray, too. Geoff's research into 2012 started about 25 years ago and was first summarized in a now-rare booklet called *Beyond 2012*. In September 2000, he compiled *2012 Dire Gnosis*, which was designed to gather more input from people all over the world. This has become the Internet's leading database on the year 2012. Jeff wouldn't necessarily be reading a channelling book, for he is a researcher and is more prone to go for historical accuracy and fact as opposed to writings from an invisible Magnetic Master from the Great Central Sun with a funny "K" name. But I like to point to Geoff's statement of what might happen in 2012.

Geoff's statements would be *opinions from a scholar*, and someone who was really knowledgeable about all the available historical information on 2012. In an interview published on YouTube, he told his opinion of what was to happen beyond 2012 as follows: "It may be the expansion of our perception into another realm... a new level of consciousness, a paradigm shift." So even Geoff didn't see total doom. Instead, his interpretation was that we were moving into something very different.

But Wait, There's More – Much More

Now it gets tough, and I have to turn the page in my thinking. This book is about everything I have indicated so far. There is a great shift going on and a full recalibration of everything we have become used to as old souls and Lightworkers on Earth. The year 2013 has been a marker for the beginning of a very new energy, and Kryon has given so many channellings about it that I can't even fit them all in this book! So what did I do when I discovered something else so profound that it would occupy six months of my life during 2012?

I found myself right in the middle of still another Gaia alignment, a profound one, and one I must report. Right when I thought I had this book all figured out and was ready to begin writing it, something else happened.

I landed in Chile at the end of 2010. Santiago was alive with energy and something unusual was happening. When I got to my hotel and turned on the TV, the first of 33 trapped miners was coming out of the ground. This was after weeks of being fed and medically treated through a small pipe. There was celebration in the streets and flags were waving everywhere. I was glued to the event for more than a day, as the "story of the 33" unfolded. This is significant, and I won't give away now what Kryon said about all this, because it's presented in full in a source I'll give you in a moment. It represents the revealed channellings when our *2012 Kundalini Tour* visited that exact site in the Chilean desert. More people watched that event in 2010 than the moon landing!

What I didn't know and would put together later is what was really beginning to happen in South America and around the earth. It would come to me powerfully in Peru a full year later, and I would hear of it over and over as I spoke to the indigenous people in the area.

The Journey of the Feathered Serpent

When Kryon visited the United Nations in 1998, he spoke of creating an *Indigenous Council of Elders*. Here are his words at that time:

"There has never been a greater time for you to implement a Council of Wisdom, a nonvoting council of indigenous Human Beings on this planet to reside in this building. And we are telling you that the consciousness of the building will eventually support this. The consciousness of the people will support it. The consciousness of the planet is pushing you toward it. It is the next logical step – and when you present it, present it to the public first. They will do the rest to help you to implement it."

   –   *Kryon to The United Nations, 1998*

The UN is not very good at grasping wise ideas and acting on them, and usually all we see is political rhetoric from the grand assembly and very few actual decisions. What most people don't realize is that the 20,000 employees of the UN spend most of their time saving the lives of children. They are responsible for millions of kids being saved through programs that eradicate disease and bring clean water and food to places you would never want to visit. But politically, they are often seen as kind of stuck. Still, I go there and channel every time I'm asked, since it brings a good energy to the halls of that building in New York City.

Some months later, Woody Vaspra, a pure Hawaiian and honored elder in the Lakota tribe of North America, decided to work toward this goal. He visited many elders, and his story is told in Kryon Book Eight, *Passing the Marker* (Chapter 14). One of the subjects in his article was called, "The Journey of the Feathered Serpent". I should have paid more attention, for right there in my own Kryon book was the revelation of the future of the planet.

The article told of the movement of the Kundalini of the earth, as given by the indigenous of the planet. It was a movement of energy from north to south, giving the earth a new balance of consciousness. It would begin happening in the 18 years leading up to 2012, the years of the great shift.

The Prophecy of the Eagle and the Condor

It was only a few years before 2012 when a very odd thing began to happen. All over the planet, the indigenous people were stirring. Unknown to most of us, they were comparing notes, and their elders were meeting with other elders. These tribes of indigenous people normally don't mingle much. Instead, they have their own unique ceremonies, their own issues with white culture, and their own beliefs. Suddenly, however, there was a common denominator, but they were somewhat quiet about it.

They realized that their prophecies about 2012 and beyond were almost identical. This prophecy spoke of the cycle of 500-year segments (Remember the Mayan discussion above? *Pachacuti* was the name given to those segments.). The end of one of those segments is 2012, and it basically was the Prophecy of the Eagle and the Condor.

THE PROPHECY: If humanity makes it past the 2012 alignment, a rebalancing of the planet would begin. The Northern Hemisphere, known as the Masculine Hemisphere, would begin to balance for the first time with the Southern Hemisphere, known as the Feminine Hemisphere. The symbolism would be the meeting of the Eagle and the Condor. Other prophecies about other Pachacuti segments had told of the potential conquerors from the north (representing Spain). They were all right on.

Their prophecy spoke the same information that Woody Vaspra had given in my Kryon book through his affiliation with the Lakota.

The Journey of the Feathered Serpent was part of it, but it was now being repeated over and over, and many had different names for it. When we were in Peru, a famous and well-respected Shaman told us that the whole area was feeling, "the awakening of the puma". It seemed that everywhere we went, there was something happening and aware people knew that a shift was beginning.

Back to The Indigenous People

Tribes from all over the planet were beginning to get together. Many elders from widely separated areas were forming kinds of committees where they could agree to meet and celebrate the shift. One was called "The Roots of the Earth" which started meeting in Central America for the first time in 2005. Hundreds came. The Hopi, Lakota, and other tribes whose names I don't know gathered from the north and the south to celebrate the Prophecy of the Eagle and the Condor (www.raicesdelatierra.org).

Don Alejandro, a Mayan elder (The Grand Elder Grandfather), was also involved in creating a giant impact in awareness of the same prophecy. His spirit name is *Wakatel Utiw* (Wandering Wolf). He was instrumental in creating a movie called, "The Shift of the Ages". His work is mainly on YouTube and well documented on the web. *Google* it to see just how big it is, or see it at www.shiftoftheages.com.

As I write this section of the book, I'm in Colombia, South America, and here I have met a man who is part of still another awakening group who has discovered the same thing, and he reports that these groups are also meeting in Europe.

The meetings continue to this day, all centered around a grand truth, one I had never heard about before. Imagine, the grandest prophecy of all, one hinted at by Kryon, was never really exposed until now. We were too consumed by our western ways and our western prophecies to even notice. But more than that, this grand prophecy was about an amazing shift of positive influence. It wasn't about doom, so it didn't have a chance in the media. Now it does. You are reading about it here.

Back to the Prophecy

I want you to realize and understand the significance of this prophecy. It's the reason Kryon and many others are here. It centers around the very message that Kryon gave in 1989, and one that can be read in Kryon Book One, *The End Times*. Kryon started that book by telling us that there would be no doom at the millennium. He told us there would be no world war, as scripture had indicated. He told us that the very energy of humanism would change. He told us that the magnetics would shift (they did). He told us the weather would change (it has!). All of these things are adding up to one great realization: We are beginning a full recalibration of everything we have ever known. Everything.

The prophecy goes on to describe that the wisdom of the planet will recenter itself from the north to the south. This is not an actual movement of wisdom, but rather a realignment of it. For centuries, the Northern Hemiphere has seen its wisdom center classically within the areas of Tibet and India. This is where Gregg Braden has done a great deal of his research, and also where he has discovered libraries filled with ancient writings that the earth has not yet seen publicly.

When you look at what has happened in those areas, you see an old energy that actually tried to sequester these writings. This is what happens when unbalance is prevalent and duality is strong. It has been the way of things as long as we have been recording history. The Dalai Lama knows he is never going home, but he also *knows* that his next reincarnation may have a chance to return. He knows about the rebalance.

This rebalance is then a realignment of the wisdom of Tibet and India that will gently sweep down to the areas of Bolivia and Peru. It will center itself in the areas of Lake Titicaca and the Island of the Sun. (Lake Titicaca belongs to both Bolivia and Peru.) It also will encompass areas that are close by, such as Machu Picchu and some of the Andes mountains of South America. Many indigenous people have called this realignment "the movement of the Kundalini" of the planet.

The Kundalini metaphor is a good one, but many people love to apply the rules of 3D to all of this esoteric information. They look for planetary chakras, locations where the movement is now, and so on and so forth. Some even asked, *"Can this movement get past the ditch we built in Panama?"* Kryon has given channellings about this, and they are published (more on this later). This is energy, not an army. So you can't measure any of the attributes of it on the surface of the earth. It's not some physical thing snaking its way from north to south.

Some have asked, *"Well, what will Tibet do without its wisdom anymore?"* This is funny; we tend to think in such a linear 3D way! Tibet will lose nothing, and the wisdom that was there will increase and rebalance! This realignment is about a full change in the planet and a realignment of all wisdom. The wisdom that was always in South America will now awaken fully, thereby changing the balance. Understand?

Ignore the idea of a physical journey of energy from Tibet to Bolivia for a moment and instead think of a pot of water that is starting to change temperature on the stove. As the cold water begins to heat up, would you look at the pot and ask, *"Where is the temperature now? Is it travelling from one area of the pot to another?"* No. All the water is involved in changing. It's the same with this realignment. It works on the entire earth, and Gaia is greatly involved.

It affects the Crystalline Grid and all Human consciousness. It is "heating up the earth with balanced wisdom".

The Kundalini is a metaphor for spiral movement and procreation. It's only a metaphor and it came from the indigenous people who constantly work in metaphors. It signals a new birth and the movement associated with a realignment of structure to allow for birth. In this case, the birth is of an energy within Gaia and humanity that has not occurred before.

The Kryon team has been celebrating this Kundalini rebalance by going to sacred places in South America. In some very profound tours and cruises starting in 2012, we circled southern South America (Cape Horn) in what is called Patagonia. Beginning in Buenos Aires, Argentina, and ending in Santiago, Chile, we did a 12-day cruise. We continued with a tour that lasted more than 30 days in cars and buses, boats and airplanes. We crossed the Andes and visited four countries, travelling to the most amazing spiritual places on Earth. We felt the new energy profoundly. We were met by the guardians of the canyons and mountains, who spoke to us through Kryon. We realized the Pleiadian connection was alive and well, and we "heard" through a multitude of Kryon channellings about the awakening that was happening throughout the area.

We sat on the top of the Island of the Sun at Lake Titicaca at an altitude of 4,000 meters (13,123 ft) and felt the incredible serenity of the lake and surrounding mountains while Kryon channelled the reality of the Prophecy of the Eagle and the Condor. I felt the whisper of the Ancients and the gentle love of Gaia as I began to channel within a field of grass at the base of the highest mountain in the Andes (Mt. Aconcagua). I stood and channelled on a ledge overlooking Machu Picchu, where Kryon talked about the Awakening of The Puma – the Peruvians knew what Kryon was talking about.

During the 2012 "Kryon Kundalini Tour" 28 channellings were given. We recorded them wherever we were, using battery power or whatever we had for electricity. We subjected our equipment to dirt, wind, water, and the heat of the sun. Months later, I had to replace almost all of the electronics, even the microphone! But it was worth it, and the recordings were placed on my Kryon website as fast as we could get to civilization where there was an Internet connection. Want to see this journey on a 9-minute free video? Go to www.kryon.com/kundalinitour.

The 33

In the desert of Chile, our bus took a long journey over dirt roads to a prearranged appointment with owners of a mining company. We went to the exact place where the 33 miners were rescued in 2010. This is a profound metaphor for the birth of mother energy in South America and, according to Kryon, is the FIRST MASS COMPASSIONATE EVENT that has affected the planet, but that represents the energy of joy and celebration, instead of sorrow, death, and horror. This rescue actually set off the monitors at the Global Consciousness Project - Princeton University (http://noosphere.princeton.edu) and was measured on the Global Coherence Initiative satellites (www.glcoherence.org/monitoring-system/about-system.html).

For those who don't know, these are the same systems that have reported compassionate events from the death of Princess Diana in 1997, the 9/11 attacks of 2001, and the Indian Ocean tsunami event of 2004. I am referring to scientific experiments that I have reported on in previous books. These experiments have shown that coherence of thought from millions of people actually changes geomagnetic measurements of the planet and creates "patterning" of random number generators set to measure exactly these things. The energy of compassion changes the planet!

Kryon said that this was the beginning of the recalibration of how the earth will operate in the future, where compassionate action will be the catalyst for major shift. He also told us that the planet will begin to react to positive things in the same way it has previously done with disaster. The Chilean mine rescue was just the first of many of these kinds of "compassionate events".

You can't ignore the number 33! In Kryon Book 12, I wrote an entire chapter devoted to the energy of numbers and the science of numerology. The system I referred to was the ancient Tibetan system, and it has the number 33 as the "last identified master number" in current numerology. A master number is two identical numbers side-by-side, such as 11, 22, 33, 44, etc. However, 44 through 99 have no identified meanings in that ancient system. According to the Ancients, we are not yet evolved enough to have those numbers be relevant to our energy. So the 33 is significant, and when you start to look at what actually happened over those weeks, it's astonishing!

In the numerology system I studied, the number 33 means, "The Compassion of the Christ". As mentioned above, it is the highest energy of any series of numbers that currently exists. The overwhelming reoccurrence of the number 33 was even noted by CNN during coverage of the event. The confluence of the appearance of this number over and over throughout the weeks of the rescue was seen by the mainstream as "bizarre". It was even reflected six months before the collapse in the timing of the earthquake (3:33 a.m.) that was said to be the contributing factor to the mine's weakness.

After the cave-in, there were 33 days of drilling before the 33 miners were found. The now famous note, which came up with the drill that broke into that dark hole in the ground 700 meters (2,300 feet) below had 33 characters in it (counting the spaces as characters). After the saga and the rescue were over, it is said that the last Human to come up from the refuge before it was sealed placed his foot on the surface at 33 minutes past midnight. There are more synchronicities of the 33 to report, a whole metaphysical story to tell, and one that you can read about in detail. Read on.

My Puzzle

So now I finally get to tell you of my quandary through 2012, a puzzle that now has found an excellent solution that has only come about in the past few months. I teach that this is how Spirit works, supplying solutions at the last moment.

For over a year, Kryon has been giving wonderful information about everything I have been reporting to you as you have read these opening pages. If you go to the free audio page on my website, you can see my quandary. Take a look at the number of channellings that were given in 2012 here: [www.kryon.com/freeaudio]. The amount of information is amazing, and it would fill at least two complete books with channelling and information about what is happening right now, and this doesn't even include the channellings being given in 2013. But I only can do one book. *"Kryon, what do I do? What do I leave out?"*

There are really two complete subjects represented on my audio pages for 2011 and 2012, and a plethora of information and channelling about both of them. The two subjects are (1) the recalibration of the energy of the planet for the new energy (Human Being-related information) and (2) the movement of the Kundalini and The Prophecy of the Eagle and the Condor (Gaia-related information). Which one should I do for Kryon Book 13? The solution was delivered to me in 2012.

I would like to introduce you to the first Kryon-related book that isn't one of mine! *The Gaia Effect – The Remarkable System of Collaboration Between Gaia and Humanity* is also a 2013 release (Ariane Editions). This book, by Australian author and naturalist

Monika Muranyi, is a compilation of everything that Kryon has ever channelled about Gaia! It is something I never would have had time for, and it includes new channellings from Kryon that have never been published. So it includes all the new information about the Kundalini movement and even the channellings given during the South American Kundalini tour!

This is an amazing job of research, listening to every Kryon channelling available and reading all the Kryon books, plus all the questions and answers online. Add to that, she posed over 30 new questions, which are answered by Kryon in her book – answers that have never been seen before. Many of the audio channellings from 2012 are presented as "refreshed information" (Kryon often channels more information when transcriptions are made from the audio). This book is actually the first of three books for three specific subjects that all feature Kryon as the central information core.

Naturally, when I gave permission for her to use the words of Kryon for such a work, I was very involved. I cooperated fully in my desire to have Kryon channel the answers to profound questions, knowing all along that this new book of hers would be the answer I needed to concentrate on my own recalibration subject. All this effort took some months and many emails.

This new book from Ms. Muranyi, in my mind, completely answers the puzzle about what is happening with the movement of the Kundalini of the planet and is packed with new Kryon material. It also has the full story of the 33 miners, as told by our Chilean host, Jorge Bianchi.

Her efforts now free me to write the recalibration story, as chan-nelled by Kryon, for the book you are holding. So, reader, now there are two books for 2013 that feature the Kryon material given over the years. The Gaia book is available on the Kryon website, in the same place you will find the other Kryon books. Visit her website too: [www.monikamuranyi.com]

Let the Book Begin

If you skip back and look at the table of contents, you know that this book is intense with *recalibration information*. Even the basic energy of our life on the planet is coming under scrutiny as the subject of massive change is presented.

This information is far, far different from any information yet given in any Kryon book. In fact, it's a reboot of everything from how love works, to how dark and light are changing, to our relationship to Spirit, our relationship to Gaia, what real wisdom looks like, what the future may hold, and the changes in our personal lives in the next 18 years.

This is the reason Kryon is here. I know that now. In the last 20 or so years, we have slogged through incredibly old energy attributes to get to this point. The darkness doesn't want to lose a battle that it has been in control of for centuries, and it's going to fight to the end to keep everything the same. However, in the face of this, the Ancients have told us that this is the time where the dark and light will begin to balance in a way that will begin a process Kryon has told us about for more than 23 years. We are approaching the possibility of a very slow change of consciousness, a recalibration of everything, even the things most sacred to us. Change is upon us, but without the darkness of the old battle we have been fighting all this time.

The attributes of a heavy energy have battled the Lightworker ever since Kryon arrived. We have been told to doubt almost everything Kryon has taught by those who would "take doom to the bank". In 1993, Kryon was attacked nationally by (ready?) a Lightworker! Even the New Age started to split over the kinds of new, fresh information that was being presented. Kryon Book One stated (and I paraphrase), *You have changed the future. The consciousness of humanity will shift and the magnetic grid will move (it did). You are preparing for the real potential of peace on Earth. Contrary to all the prophecies of the past, you are going to move through the year 2000 and create a new paradigm for the planet. There will be no Armageddon and no projection of doom as you have been told for centuries.* This was more than 20 years ago.

The drama engine, represented both in the New Age and non New Age, didn't like this. There simply was too much money to be made in keeping things working by promoting fear. There were too many people invested in "hanging on to gurus" and giving away their power to spiritual leaders who told them, *"This is the only truth. Follow me or perish, since you can't know what I know. Stay in my compound and give me your wealth."* But now all this starts to change.

Old souls have gone through so many personal energy shifts during this time! We have experienced small wars on the planet that made us wonder if the old energy was winning. We have had terror attacks that were so horrific that they changed the entire future of air travel. We've seen children gunned down in their schools and journalists beheaded on live TV and in the street. Is it possible that things would ever change? Can Human nature ever shift past this?

Well, get ready for the same kind of thing that happened in 1989 when Kryon first arrived. Within two years of his original message, the Soviet Union officially dissolved (1991), sending the prophecies of centuries into the wastebasket of time.

Kryon has predicted much over these 23 years. In Chile in 2008, he told an audience to get ready for significant movement of the earth a bit south of where they were sitting. It happened just as he told them, with the massive 8.8 Chilean earthquake of 2010, just south of where Kryon had given the message. Kryon gave the prediction of the potential revolution in Iran, and it started within a year of his words being published, but was squashed immediately. By the way, he continues to tell us of this revolution and says it "remains the potential of Iran's future".

So we are at yet another crossroads, where Kryon is again giving rebellious New Age information at a time when many can only see negativity. But now it's different. We have 20 years of evidence that perhaps the messages of Kryon are accurate and true, and that even though this book is filled with unbelievable predictions about an earth that is starting to correct itself, it can happen. This time it's more believable, because we are actually starting to observe the shift. Perhaps this time there won't be the drama and opposition from those who need things to stay the same. Perhaps this time, they might even join us instead of fighting us? This is my dream.

Enjoy this book, dear ones. Kryon is again telling us about a future that has not been seen yet or predicted yet, but that is starting to unfold before our eyes. Along the way, I'll guide each channelling with a few words or experiences that I wish you to have.

Lee Carroll

"Count the dictators on the planet, dear ones, and compare that number to a few years ago. Take a look at what the citizens of certain countries have decided they want and don't want after centuries of living in 'sameness.' Count the efforts to unite countries and economies, then compare that to the small number who wish to make war or create separation and fear. Count the number of old energy leaders who are afraid right now of what is happening on the planet and of losing their power. Sit for a moment and contemplate these things. For no matter what you are told, you can look out the window and see the light coming. Let the reality of what is actually taking place replace the words of those who want to convince you to follow them into their dark places. Let the love of God give you the discernment of the ages, old soul, for this is your responsibility and your legacy in these new days of your awakening planet."

Kryon

May - 2013

It Begins...

This is the first channelling of 2012, and it's where Kryon begins to describe how we are going to feel from here on. Although 2013 is the marker where we really begin all this, Kryon starts letting us know what to expect way in advance. Personally, I didn't really think the energy would be all that different – until I got to 2013 and things started to shift. It was because of these 2012 channellings that I did something I never would have done. I decided to cancel the Kryon flagship event in 2013, the Kryon Summer Light Conference. Now I know why I did.

Lee Carroll

Chapter One

THE RECALIBRATION OF THE HUMAN BEING
Red Deer, Alberta, Canada
January 2012

Kryon
Book 13

Chapter One
The Recalibration of the Human Being
Live Kryon Channelling - January 2012

Greetings, dear ones, I am Kryon of Magnetic Service. The attribute of those from the other side of the veil is compassion. There are always questions, however. Some ask, *"How do I know who is visiting me? I'm afraid of this or that and when I channel and I open my mouth, I don't know what's going to happen. Do I allow any energy in the universe to pop in?"* And we say to you, oh, how 3D of you to think that the angels standing around you would ever let that happen! If it's compassionate energy, it is from God. If it is not, it is from you. It's that simple. Do not envision in your mind a plethora of dark energies waiting to pounce upon you, for this is a man-made suggestion. You've humanized God so much that you're not even sure when Spirit takes your hand!

Let tonight change that. Know that wherever you go, you could call it what you wish, but there is a grand entourage with you. It's a beautiful system.

2012

I want to talk about what is currently happening on the planet and I would like to give you, in this, the first full channelling of 2012, what I would call the attributes of the energy visiting you now. This energy is changing.

After my explanation, old souls will know more about the experiences that they are having and will understand more about what is causing them. This is given in love and there's no fearful thing here. You sit in a safe place.

The energy that is being visited upon this earth has been expected. The Ancients predicted it and we have given you recent channellings, even the channeling given in that country which you call Peru, about the shift of what we would call the movement of the feathered serpent [first presented in Kryon, Book 8 in 2000]. There's an actual polarity shift happening between the male and female energy of the planet. The Northern Hemisphere, which has always been masculine-heavy, is changing. The Southern Hemisphere, which has not been biased in that way, is changing. The wisdom of the Ancients in the Southern Hemisphere is beginning to replace the wisdom of the Ancients in the North. And you're starting to see a softer Human Being.

Spiritually, the old souls are alerted to this shift first and are beginning to receive biological changes. You expected it and it's here. This process is being felt by the entire planet. Those disruptions you see in countries right now, which have not had disruptions for hundreds of years, are a result of this change – for this is what takes place when humanity begins to have more compassion, when they wish to unify more than be separate, and new thoughts and wisdom start to occur.

New Invention

This new consciousness creates new inventions – higher science, higher thinking and solutions to those things that you have called basic Human issues. Population explosion, food, water, power generation – all of these things are going to change. There will be new thinking, new thought and new revelation in the next two generations, some of it even in the next 18 years. But a shift is occurring and I want to tell you who's going to feel it first. It's those in the chairs, listening to my voice and reading this, who have been on this planet so many times that they are used to the old energy. Old soul, you're starting to *remember*. You're starting to remember what it used to be like and what it can be like again. Old soul, you are beginning to *recalibrate* and this is cellular change in 3D.

These energy shifts we speak of are not going to be some kind of New Age esoteric magic. Instead, you're going to see them clearly grounded in governments and in science. You're going to see it all over the planet as energy begins to shift away from what anyone expected. Slowly. I've said it before. Slowly - There'll be countries that have been in isolation for years that will open their gates. You better take some pictures now, because things will never be the same. Slowly, they will join the rest of you, and their children will meet your children and you'll realize you have things in common and not the low energy attributes that you have been told.

The Recalibration of Biology

The recalibration of the old soul is the subject of this and tomorrow's channel. So the channels will be similar and not a continuation. You don't need Part A and Part B. I'll give you everything today and everything tomorrow. I want you to know what you can expect and what some of you are already working with: Recalibration. Your biology has to shift. It has to absorb and work with, and be part of, a softer energy. If it's going to do that, there has to be a recalibration of the core, or the center of the energy.

Those who have studied the lattice, representing the patterned energies around you, know of calibration. You know of the energies of balance that are required for a Human to start changing themselves. You know about that which is body rejuvenation, mentioned even this day about how cells divide and how every single kind of cell in your body, including brain and heart and skin, regenerates. They are designed to regenerate and if they're lost, they're designed to regenerate, and if they're damaged, they're designed to regenerate. Oh, I say it again, Human, don't you find it odd that the starfish can grow back a limb and you can't? Don't you think that's odd? This will change.

Well, if everything rejuvenates, don't you find it odd that a disease can start to change how a Human thinks, and the scientist will tell you that their brain cells are starting to die or move or change or be poisoned, and the Human even loses the memory of love? Where is the rejuvenation? Where is the repair? That's not how DNA is designed, dear ones. Cells are designed to go back to the blueprint and create a new, fresh cell. That's how it's designed! Your science is going to see that and your spiritual bodies are going to see that, and the ones who sit in the chairs have got to recalibrate to work with it.

The recalibration is automatic. You don't have to ask for it. Let me repeat that. It's going to happen because you're an old soul, and that's why you're here. You don't have to ask for it. But the recalibration is what you expected and what you're remembering. But perhaps it's not what you expect, exactly?

It's uncomfortable! Now some of you will know where this message is going when we start giving you the attributes that I would say are less than positive, which some of you will experience in the recalibration process. Now, this is some of you, not all. Every single Human Being has their own unique path, so they will experience these things in their own way. So this is not a generic list of what is going to happen to all old souls. These are, instead, potentials of many symptoms of recalibration that old souls may experience, and who are here and ready to move forward on this planet.

The List

Some of you will have dizziness. It's an attribute of recalibration. That's all it is and it will pass. But it's worrisome, for those who will become dizzy will also become disoriented and that might even cause a fall. So what do you do with this new knowledge? Number one – know you're not catching a horrible brain disease. Number two – walk more carefully! Does that make sense to you?

There are other things. You're going to have trouble sleeping – more trouble than normal. You're not going to have one awakening, but rather two or more. So already some of you, who have been feeling these things, know what's going on. It's recalibration.

The first question the Human asks is, *"How long will this occur?"* The answer is, as long as it takes, oh dense one. [Kryon smile] I think you get the idea. The recalibration will take place as long as it takes, and if you fight it, it will take longer. Worse yet, if you drug yourself against it, it's just going to keep happening. Celebrate it and move forward with it. Tell your cellular structure you understand and move with it, not against it. This will quicken it and it will pass even sooner.

Every single biology [Human] in the room is different, and now we bring up something that we have not brought up for some time, but you need to hear it. What works for you in health is based almost completely and totally upon your Akashic inheritance. Where did you spend the most lifetimes? Perhaps it was in Asia? Perhaps India or Tibet? Perhaps it was in the Southern Hemisphere? Each of those places and cultures will have had different food, which worked to keep you balanced and healthy. Yet, here you are in the Northern Hemisphere, in this lifetime. What I want you to know is that you are significantly influenced by the kind of diet that you used to have [in your past lives].

Perhaps you were vegan. Perhaps you ate only grains. Therefore, your cells will crave that diet to feel balanced. Do you understand? There are others who come mainly from North America, from Europe, and who never had those kinds of diets from Asia or the south. Therefore, they won't have any trouble at all with the food of the land. Listen: There is no one, generic answer to the question: *"What should I eat for Spiritual health?"* There are no absolute "shoulds." Instead, there are good signals from "innate" inside you, which gives insight as to the most healthy things for your own body. In other words, listen to your cells! [see chapter six]

Now, why do I mention this? Because you're going to get advice from people on what to eat to correct what's wrong with you as you recalibrate. So I'm going to tell you right now, ignore them. Instead, go inside and let your own Akashic Record tell you what is going to work for you. Don't be surprised if some of you come up allergic to some things you've always eaten. I will tell you: Your biology is recalibrating. This attribute will be necessary for you to move forward, for you to shift to the place where you can be balanced with the most wisdom.

Many of you might not like some processed food, because you're not used to it in your Akash. Do you see what I'm saying? If you're going to pull the Shamanic energy up from the depths of the wisdom that you have learned and walked through over and over through past history, some things are going to come with it – like your balanced diet, for instance – and you're going to have to deal with it. Don't fight it.

Expect these things. They're there for you to see and feel. See them for what they are: recalibration. *"Dear Spirit,"* you might say, *"thank you for this recalibration, for caring enough about me to know that this is where I want to go and what I want to do."* Human Being, how you recalibrate now will determine how you will come back in the next life. You won't have to go through this again – ever. Akashic inheritance is far more than the genealogy of those Human Beings you came from [parents]. You know this. An inherited Akash represents those things that you've experienced in all the lifetimes, regardless of your parents' genes. Sometimes, these are the most predominant and heaviest things that you have to deal with. The ones in the chairs listening to my voice are beginning to deal with these things. So that is the other thing: Expect these past things to come forward for clearing.

Clearing the Past

Maybe you haven't done very well with the life lessons in the last few lives, and you felt you would do better in this one? You will, because the earth needs you. And it doesn't need you encumbered with fear. Instead, it needs you to say to yourselves, *"I accept this recalibration. No matter what is in my body at this moment, it can be gone. If it's inappropriate, it can be gone. I stand as a piece of divinity on this planet – wise, appropriate, and I belong here. This is my time. Cellular structure, listen: If there's anything inappropriate, let it be gone. Let it wash away with the waste. Let it go out because it is not seen as appropriate, it is not commensurate to the energy of the love of God. Let only compassionate things enter my consciousness."* This may be hard for some of you to say.

The Good News

So now, let us look at those things that you can expect physically, which will not be as hard.

Number one: You are going to be able to deal with even the worst habits that you've ever had in your life, and get rid of them very quickly. It is a new energy of cooperation with the energy of the Lightworker. Did you get that? Oh, let us pause, please, and take just a moment for a deep breath, for I am dealing with those listening to my voice and reading this who have gone through thousands of years of persecution, suffering and torture. There are those who have been burned at the stake. This is because the energy you brought into the earth was not a match at all for what the earth was experiencing. Holy men and women would be asked to heal somebody one moment, and then to go to the edge of the village and jump off a cliff the next. Fear is that way. And you're here. I know you. You've come back. However, now, this planet is starting to move so that all of the things that you have brought to this planet with your Akashic experience will begin to cooperate with the new energy.

Oh, take a deep breath, for enhanced manifestation begins – not immediately; not today; not this hour; but ever so slowly. This quantum clock starts to move in your direction. The earth is receiving a more gentle, passionate energy. That is what you were born with. That's the tool that you have. In the past, this has been seen as odd and strange and representing weakness. You've been ostracized. Some of you have been cast out of your family. I know who's here. I'm telling you that in this new energy, even they may look at you differently and see how you've started to become softer, not even knowing it's they who have changed.

Things are going to work that didn't before. Do you have a habit you'd like to break? Is it the way you think or the way you eat? Is it what you put into your body? Is it what you smoke? Is it killing you and you know it? You know who I'm talking to, dear one. Would you like to change it? I'm telling you that what you do in this energy is going to respond in your body very differently, even if you tried it before.

Listen: Not one of you is allowed to say, old soul, wise one, you're not allowed to say, *"I tried that and it didn't work."* If you do, it will be as a child talking who doesn't know how things work. Instead, you're going to say, *"This time I know better. I will manifest it because the body is listening. It's my time."*

Cooperative Energy and How to Use It

So that's what the new energy brings: Cooperation. Things are going to go better and flow better. They're going to move forward instead of back. When you put out the word for what you wish to have in your life and the process begins, many of you are going to start seeing a positive return right away. Synchronicity is the key. Put yourself in places to have those things take place. Do not try to manifest something and then go into the closet and wait for it. Instead, put yourself in places where you would expect it to manifest. Do you understand? That is where the answers will be because there are others walking around with your solution! They're looking for you, as you look for them. Don't sequester yourself. In a recalibration mode, there's a tendency to sequester, because you don't feel quite right.

The Common Cold

You're going to catch more colds, but then you're going to heal them quicker – and why would that be? The Human cold has always been a recalibration of the biological process. To catch a cold is needed, and that is why you cannot "cure" it. You must go through it. The common cold is a cyclical opportunity for the immune system to correct itself. Perhaps you didn't know that? That's why you're not going to receive the chemistry to cure the common cold. It's a recalibrating device within you. It builds up the system in a certain way that helps you, and it must be recurring. Don't be shocked when you catch one, and say, *"Well, I didn't think that would happen because I just got through with the other one."* It's recalibration.

These are the kinds of things we wanted to bring to you, so that you will know what is taking place and not fear it. There are many positive things representing a truly positive energy that is occurring on the planet and turning the corner of opportunity for humanity. This is an energy that supports the Lightworker. There's no more upstream swim, dear ones.

Now, all of you are different, and I know who you are. Commitment is the key. You cannot do any of these things casually, but you knew that, didn't you? When you commit to the manifestation of what you need in your life, the Universe is listening. When you receive messages from my side of the veil, I will tell you something that you already may know. We do not have a clock. So I speak to you in the *now*.

I see the energy in the room, and I see who is here. I see the old soul. I speak to you in the *now*. So it's up to you what your clock does and how long it takes in your reality. In my reality, it's already done, already accomplished, for the strongest potentials become manifested reality. Can you see that way? Can you walk out of here with it already done in your mind? There's energy in this room that is infusing itself right now into the places it needs to go.

What to Expect Spiritually

Spiritually, what can you expect? This recalibration is about being able to stay on this planet in health and in happiness without drama or fear. That is what the old soul remembers as the potential of this time.

[Pause]

My partner mentioned earlier in his communications [the lecture] that one of the greatest mysteries to him is why old souls have such profound self-worth issues. In his ignorance, he stands there and says he has no idea why this would be with old souls. I'll tell you why: It's because for hundreds of years, you've been beat up! Every time you move two steps forward, you're beat back one – sometimes five. Then you come into this life expecting what? Very little. For some of you to even start a project, you have the little voice inside that says, *"Oh, I knew that would happen."* You don't expect much, do you? That's because in an older energy, everything you did was met with resistance. Everything. Every time you wanted to make a positive suggestion about something that might help, you were told to get lost. Every time you saw spiritual wisdom in a complicated problem, nobody else saw it. They weren't interested. You were isolated over and over. When things got hot, you called for a solution. Most others called for the sword. Now we are saying that this is changing.

So, spiritually you are going to have to love yourself more, and now is your opportunity to do so because there is a Universe inside of you called cellular structure with trillions of pieces of DNA. These pieces are starting to react and are becoming ready for your instruction sets to be given. The hand is out, you might say, of your cellular structure, and the cells are saying, *"Ok, you're the boss. What are we going to do?"*

The Key to Self-worth

Self-worth is a program. It's a program! It's information developed from experience, and it's something that is learned. You can un-program it! All you have to do is tell yourself what you want. *"Dear cellular structure,"* you might say, *"I deserve to be here. This is my time. I have things that others want. This is my time. I'm important in the scheme of the earth. I have earned my stripes. This is my time. Dear cellular structure, get rid of inappropriate, emotional issues that keep me from moving forward into my beauty and power. The power that I speak of is that ability to create compassion and light everywhere I go."*

Your cellular structure will smile, give you the hand that has been waiting, and say, "We are your partner in this co-creation. Let's get going."

Uncomfortable?

Recalibration. It's going to have attributes that are challenging and that are beautiful. What's it going to feel like to you, to suddenly become more enlightened and have more information? You will feel you're much more part of God – with a cold. [Kryon smile] Falling over sometimes, and you have to laugh. Biology is this way. It takes a while for the shift - months, perhaps more.

So while you deal with the issues of recalibration and discomfort, know why they are here. Then at the same time, celebrate that which is in you, which is more compassion and which starts to work in your life. Things are going to work better.

Free Will and the Whole Picture

Now, all this is assuming that you get this message and you relate to it and manifest it. That is to say, your free will choice is what's going to happen. If you ignore the message, very little will happen. You're still an old soul and you have free choice.

Finally, I give you one of the common questions about this recalibration: *"Kryon, you say the Earth energy is shifting. That means all humanity is going to feel it. Right?"* Yes. All humanity will feel it. You're going to see it in the way governments are eliminated and are re-formed. You're going to see it in ways of different thinking. You're going to see it in the ways my partner has told you are possible, which I have channelled in the past, thinking differently.

Old energy regimes will not renew themselves, but decide to change. Societies that have lasted 1,000 years a certain way will decide to suddenly change. Cooperation and unity over the next two generations will start to become the norm. Someday there will come a time where you will look back on today and say, *"We were barbarians."* That's a change.

Timing and the Future

I am on my side of the veil in the *now*. I have no clock to give you here. I am just telling you that this is what I see. I see a healed planet, eventually with new science. I see a planet where there is no permanent disease and where clean water is never an issue. Never! I see a time where all Humans have electricity and it's easy to get and it's inexpensive, where you can heat your homes easily and well. These are all of the things that are in the strongest potentials in the quantum soup of manifestation. But I cannot give you a clock.

What I *can* tell you is that as Earth recalibrates itself there are going to be issues. Some of them will be political, and some will get worse in the recalibration attributes, and the Earth will feel it.

Will everyone become enlightened? No. You represent less than one-half of one percent of the Human population, old soul, and you are going to strike that match in the dark. We've told you this before: You've become the match bearer in the dark when a few lights allow all to see better. That's your job, only the work just got easier.

I speak in the *now*. I cannot give you a clock. Please understand the wisdom of this as you leave the room. See the potentials, not the daily news, and if things don't happen tomorrow, Human Being, in your quick turn-around consciousness, don't be angry. God has patience; you have patience. Isn't it worth it, having lived all these lives, to now come and give this one a chance?

There are those in this room who wonder how long they're going to live, because of what's going on right now. You know who I'm talking to. So I will tell you the potential that I see is a very long life. There are still those who might say to me, "*Yeah but, yeah but, yeah but...*" No matter what I tell you, some will have an excuse why it can't work. That is the old energy speaking to you. Recalibrate! Start seeing what is possible and make it what IS.

The Quantum Factor

Finally, this: The more science takes a look at atomic structure in the very small and then looks at the Universe in the very large, they will begin to see a commonality. Your science is starting to see that there's no randomness in what looks to be random in 3D. Instead, they're looking at *intelligent design*. This means that in those attributes you call *creation*, the way things came together were biased for life, biased for compassion. What you see is the handiwork of God. It can no longer be denied that there is a Creator.

As you turn inward and start to deal with yourselves, I want you to see the same thing within you. It's about time you understand that you are not random. Your life is not random. Things don't happen to you randomly. They happen to you in a way that you create. There is a system here, and it can be directed and programmed and re-programmed. This is manifestation.

This is the lesson of all humanity eventually – to create a healed earth, to create a peaceful one, to go places you never dreamed you would go in invention and health. This is the beginning. I have no clock. But I have the strongest potentials to see, and that is what I give you today as my partner sits in the chair in front of you. The potentials that we see are grander than they were last year. If the Lightworkers will recalibrate easily, they can speed the process. Don't fight it.

So, as you leave this place and life returns to normal, and the routine is the routine, you might look back upon these few minutes we've had together and say, *"I wish I could do those things."* You tend to fall back into the old energy so easily, not realizing who you are. This is why recalibration is needed, so you will not think that way. What happens in a multi-dimensional state has to do with consciousness out of time and space. Just walking on this planet, holding the light, creates energy that you did not know you had. That's why we want you to stay in health, without drama or fear. Those who feel they are not doing anything for the planet are in a black and white world as they spread color all around.

So assign a goal, if you wish, because Humans love to do that. But let me tell you this: There are many of you already achieving change just by being alive and having compassion for others around you. Some of you in the room are teachers; some are channellers, and some are healers. Some are not interested, and I know who they are as well, for this message is not for all. You stand on a precipice of potential that I came here for. That's why Kryon is here – to help you across this bridge. Congratulations for making it this far.

The old energy will fight back, dear ones. Expect that, but this time expect to win. And you will. For now, in 2012, is the beginning of Lightworkers having the upper hand. That is to say, light is being seen and the seeds that were planted so long ago are beginning to be harvested.

And so it is.

Kryon

Stand by for a science channelling!

It's one of Kryon's favorite things to do, talking about physics, and in this seminar, Dr. Todd Ovokaitys is present. Kryon loves to interview Dr. Todd, since he has identified him as a Lemurian priest of note. So if you don't mind some science, you will enjoy this channelling. If you don't like science, wade through this anyway, for in the next chapter, I have a gift for you – a never-before-seen snapshot of what it's like when I sit in the chair and channel. The intensity of it all might surprise you.

Lee Carroll

Chapter Two
THE RECALIBRATION OF KNOWLEGE
Boulder, Colorado
January 2012
Kryon
Book 13

Chapter Two
The Recalibration of Knowlege
Live Kryon Channelling - January 2012

Greetings, dear ones, I am Kryon of Magnetic Service. We have only a few things to say, but it's going to require that we do it slowly and accurately, for we're dealing with things my partner has no knowledge of. So I give him intuitive visions, and he then translates them in real time as he receives them. Even the voice that you hear, the consciousness that you perceive, and the energy that is around him are his ability to meld with Spirit in a quantum state. This allows him to bring forward in what you call real time a message that he is not aware of. He steps aside as he does now and, with curiosity, listens to what's happening next. It is not a *takeover.*

The man who is in the chair and I have an agreement, and it's one he hasn't talked about much. Years ago when I said to him, "We are going to channel in this fashion," he said, *"I refuse to have a takeover."* So instead, I offered him a meld and I said to him, "If you will meld with me during these times, there will come a day when the meld is permanent." And he agreed. Then he asked me, *"Is the meld unusual?"* I told him no. It is what every single Human can do – not to sit in front of Humans and channel as you see now, but instead to have a direct portal to the Creator in all things. It isn't unusual. In fact, it's what every Human on Earth intuitively feels they want – a connection to home.

These things have been done by Humans many times before, and before that they were done, and before that they were done [explained in a channelling to come later]. The result of doing the meld properly eventually connects you to the Creative source and you stop being a *Human,* as you define it.

The ones who seeded this planet walk this day here and they don't die. They're in a quantum state and they can travel wherever they want. They reside in certain parts of the earth, including Mt. Shasta and Hawaii [in your country] and many other portals on the planet. Many of you reading this know what I'm talking about. And that is the promise of what happens with *earths* everywhere that go through a process where they pass the decision points and start another process, a process where they change their reality out of 3D into a new paradigm.

My Cryptic Communication

I am trying not to be cryptic, and at the same time I do not reveal the specifics of things that are not known to you yet. Spirit has a promise to humanity: Since you are the planet of free choice at the moment, we can't give you hints. All the things that are revealed must already be here in Human potential thought. All inventions of what might come about have to already be germinating somewhere in the Human mind. And if it isn't so, we don't speak of it. This respects the process of the test that is before you and the experience you have come to have. It's *your* agreement with us.

Perhaps this is the first time you've heard this from a channeller, the fact that we do not reveal things that are not already here in some form. It's the truth. However, typically Human creative thought, even of invention, of potential, of philosophy, may take a decade or more to reach the place where the masses may hear about it. So today I'm going to tell you some things that we see the potentials of that are there already. It isn't fortune telling. It's on the earth already. So I will quicky walk you through some things.

The New Energy 2012 and Beyond

You're in a new energy and it's just starting. It's different from the past *New Energy*. The end of 2011, mushing into this 2012 year, brought about what we have been predicting to you for a long time.

It is *The Bridge of Swords*. The Bridge of Swords we have described before is a bridge that humanity uses to go from one energy to another, and it's celebrated all over the Universe. It's celebrated by those who helped seed the planet and by those who helped seed them, and the ones before them and the ones before them. They are standing around you, in front of you, in the corridor of your life, crossing the swords above your head, celebrating a victory. Like the ceremony of marriage in the military, where the comrades in battle stand and cross the swords and you walk down the aisle, that's the Bridge of Swords and that's what you're doing.

Oh, dear ones, it may sound cryptic to you again, but these who cross those swords have gone through what you have gone through. They KNOW what is happening and where it may eventually lead you. They have been waiting for this for a very long time. There are so many from so many different parts of the Universe, and they all know.

Help With What is Currently Happening

You've got help. What happens to a planet that is starting to soften? Old souls are the Lightbearers and have been for years. They're the ones who can show the rest of the earth light in a dark place. That's what you've been doing for years, and it's been an uphill battle.

It's an overused metaphor, but one that we continue to use for simplicity. Consider that you have those on the planet who have walked in the dark for thousands of years. It's just darkness. It's not evil or mystical, but simply the absence of light. It's a darkness where humanity doesn't unify, because it is hard to do that if an entire Human race is walking in the dark. It's hard to know what to do when you can't see where you are walking. So you take care of yourself. It's about survival more than anything else – the basics.

In survival, you collect others around you for safety and comfort. You can hear them; you can sense them; you can collect that which is what you would call a group, and you huddle in the dark, metaphorically. This is the metaphor for the planet as you know it. Wars break out because you're in the dark. You can't see the others, so you fear them and prepare to always defend your reality. That's the way it has been for almost all of history. Suddenly, however, there is light.

What happens when there's light in a dark place, even a little? Suddenly, many can see to walk from here to there. Imagine having to walk in the darkness from A to B for centuries, and suddenly there is a light on the path. There is no fear about the unknown when you can see in front of you! You're free to unify, since you can see that the others are just like you! You're free to have ideas. You're free to have knowledge.

This particular message is what I told you it would be. You may call it *The Recalibration of Knowledge on the Planet.* Unknown to you, and very slowly, a softening is taking place, moving the energy of the planet more from the masculine to the feminine. That is to say, it is balancing what was unbalanced. North and South are coming together hemispherically, so that there's no longer a macho *Northern hemisphere*, but rather one which is balanced. It has to happen this way for Africa to do what it's going to do. (predictions ahead)

Look at Africa on the map and you'll know what I'm talking about. Balance must occur and it is occurring. Africa is literally going to be the "New World" within 75 years. What happens when you heal a continent and the basics are then available without the control of disease or dictators? The answer is an amazing beginning of a civilization that has no boundaries and nothing to unlearn but poverty. Watch for it and "stand back."

What happens when the earth starts to soften up and there's more light? Even the terrorists change. I invite you to watch for it, Human Being; I invite you to watch all of it. You can watch some things happen that you didn't expect. When the Soviet Union fell over, how many of you had the answers to why that took place without a civil war? It was because that old energy was no longer supportable by the Humans who lived there. There comes a time in the *physics of consciousness* where if you do not have a cooperative group of Human Beings who will agree with an old energy precept, it cannot be sustained. What happens when the majority of the world doesn't want war anymore? You are actually seeing this develop. Has anyone told you that you are "overdue" for another world war? In 3D, you are. Within the paradigm of the old energy, you are.

I want you to watch some countries. I don't have a clock [this statement is Kryon telling us that there is no time frame on his side of the veil, only potentials]. I'll just tell you, it's imminent [in Spirit's timing, this could mean as soon as a decade]. I want you to watch some countries carefully for changes. You're going to be seeing changes that are obvious and some that are not obvious [covert or assumptive]. But the obvious ones you will see sooner than not – Cuba, Korea [North], Iran, of course, and Venezuela. I want you to watch what happens when they start to realize that they don't have any more allies on Earth! Even their *brothers* who used to support them in their hatred of some are saying, *"Well, perhaps not anymore. It doesn't seem to be supporting us anymore."* Watch the synchronicities that are occurring. The leaders who have either died or are going to in the next year or so will take the old ways with them. Watch what happens to those who take their place, and remember these meetings where I described these potentials to you.

The Old Energy is Alive, But Not Happy

I want to tell you something: Old energy dies kicking and screaming. Old energy does not surrender, ever. Old energy simply dies hard and slow. There will be holdouts for a long time. There will be those who are convinced that the only way to get what they want is to create drama, war, and fear. They continue to want to spring up in places you felt were safe, and to pull you backwards with them. They hate the fact that the earth is going *soft* on them, and they continue to rattle their sabers, make threats, and make news doing it. They're not the majority, Human Being, but often they are the loudest. When you walk around in perfect health and you are feeling great except for your sore toe, what do you think about? Your SORE TOE! So then you watch your media talk about sore toes for endless hours, and you get depressed. I know you understand the metaphor.

The Weather... Again

My partner has been "against the grain" in the past few years, giving you what I have channelled about the weather. Is it global warming? No. Is it going to get better? No. This is a two-generation cycle. There will continue to be earthquakes, tsunamis, volcanoes, and storms. This is a recalibration of life in the ocean, and humanity must go through this in any way they can. This is a cycle, a known and expected one, but since you haven't gone through it in modern times, it's not well understood yet.

I would like to tell you that you have the same intuitive equipment that the animals do to keep you safe in the right place at the right time. Yet you don't believe it. Oh, you'll use the *Parking Angel*, but not the *Life Angel*. The little stuff is easy for you, but the big stuff is a mystery. It's the same process, *"Dear Spirit, where should I live? Dear Spirit, where should I go?"* Spirit is right there answering, and you perceive it as intuition. But the first thing you do is to say, *"Naw. That's me talking. No, I'm waiting for the voice in the sky. Sorry."* You still don't understand that this is how God speaks to individuals – through the little voice that holds your hand and is the first intuitive impression after a question.

Sometimes you get your answer before the question is asked because we know you're asking it. Sometimes we're so anxious to give you the answer, so excited that you would even ask, that it comes even before you ask, way before. This is guidance. That's what to expect. It comes with the territory of a rejuvenation of the planet and this is the year it starts being enhanced. Now, are you going to receive it or throw it away since "you" thought of it?

The Revelations to Come in Physics

Now, let's talk physics because we now can reveal some things, beautiful things, that are starting to occur in science and are starting to be seen and partially understood. What you have before you, the gentleman sitting on the floor, is Yawee. I know him well.

[Kryon is speaking now about Dr. Todd Ovokaitys, M.D., DNA researcher and member of the Kryon team, who sits on the floor in this live session. Dr. Ovokaitys has been identified by Kryon in the past as a great Lemurian scientist and keeper of the truths within the Lemurian *Temple of Rejuvenation*, discussed in 1994 in Kryon Book Two. He wrote the Foreword to Book Twelve.]

It's interesting, is it not, what the Akashic memory banks bring forward within a Human? Your Akash is soul memory designed to release information about your Akash as the energy of the earth changes to a measurement where it's appropriate to begin a process of revelation. Nikola Tesla created massless objects in his laboratory – what you would call anti-gravity. He knew how to transmit electricity wirelessly (by the way, through the ground, not the air), through the earth (not the atmosphere), and he was frustrated he could not prove it better. The technology was not there, but more than that, the energy of the planet, consciously, was not ready for him. He could not get past the barrier of the belief of others. By the way, he's back and so is Einstein and you'll know them when you see what they're up to.

The energy of your time is now appropriately ready for some of the theories that were before their time, which were just as accurate then as they are now. Watch for entirely new science to suddenly erupt with solutions to problems that you have been working on for years, solutions where you say, *"Why didn't they think of that before?"*

Expect cold fusion, by the way. I've told you this before. The experiment with cold fusion was accurate [speaking of the much-discounted Ponds and Fleischmann experiment in the past]. The experimenters could not repeat their discovery because they were not aware of the attribute of magnetics that was influencing their experiment [which was done in a basement with the electric utility panels around them]. They thought it was simple chemistry. It wasn't. It was an accidental discovery of physics that remains a mystery at the moment, but that combines chemistry with magnetics, which few are trying. The same thing happened to Tesla, where he was actually able to observe an object fly off the bench, but really didn't know why. He knew it had to do with the design of magnetics, but couldn't begin to do the design with the tools and technology of the day. Can you imagine such a thing? Now you understand his depression. Such is the way advancement often happens on this planet.

A Conversation with Yawee [The Name for Dr. Todd]

Todd is here and in this new energy his Lemurian Akash is starting to reveal what he knows. The energy moves forward and releases engrams into his consciousness. He doesn't get everything all at once, none of you do. The vision that he had started his quest, [speaking of his DNA vision years ago], but he is now remembering items that are being released to him little by little.

My messages to Yawee about his profound pineal tonings did not come from the ethers. He already knew it. But let us say, he needed a prodding so that he would match the clock of 2012. [Laughter] And it had worked and he will be ready on time. But he knew this information already. He already had the inkling and perception of the tones put together, because he knows about the cycle of physics that nobody talks about... and so we will today.

The Temple of Rejuvenation

As Yawee, Todd ran something called the Temple of Rejuvenation in Lemuria. There were attempts to recreate it in Atlantis much, much later, but that didn't work because Yawee wasn't there. Yawee had an attribute that the Lemurians knew was unusual, and that was that he lived three times the lifetime span that they did. So he had within him some secrets about energy, specifically DNA. In the Temple of Rejuvenation he had discovered something that is in the works of being discovered right now. I don't have a clock. How soon? You'll see.

So I address Yawee now in order to continue the teaching: Good morning, Yawee. [Note that the time of day is irrelevant, seeing as how this meeting was approaching 5 p.m. Many never noticed this. It's Kryon humor.]

Todd: *Good day, Magnetic Master.*

We've spoken before. We've done it like this and we've done it in private. You're not being put on the spot, for we always give these discussions in appropriate love, in order to perhaps press issues that are already there, so they match your clock [again, speaking of 3D time]. What do you remember about the Temple of Rejuvenation that comes to you in certain aspects? Do you remember what the energies were there?

Todd: *There was the use of the intrinsic magnetic core of the earth that was especially concentrated in certain areas and was further augmented by altitude.*

You remember, dear ones, listening to this and reading this, that the Temple of Rejuvenation rested on the top of Lemuria's mountain. Lemuria is the highest mountain on the planet. To this day, it remains the highest mountain, but today it is submerged. It is called Hawaii. The Islands of Hawaii are only the mountaintops of one giant mountain. Measured from the bottom to the top, it is the largest on the planet. There is snow at the top, even now. Can you imagine it 20,000 feet higher? Can you imagine what it looked like observable from space? This is the one that the Pleiadians chose to come to first. Obvious, it was.

Yawee, you might remember, you were always cold. Always cold. For you couldn't have a heater in the temple because then it didn't work! When you saw that which is being done in science today on the screen that my partner brought [a video that Lee showed earlier on macro-entanglement], did you see anything interesting that you might remember?

We speak of temperature. We speak of cold that is so cold that it actually creates less resistance to the flow of energy. This is actually the catalyst for increasing that which is magnetic by 10, 100 times, even 1,000-fold depending on the temperature. Without technical machinery, it was one of the attributes that allowed you to do what you did in that temple.

I want to ask you this: How much do you remember about the physical apparatus that was necessary for this? I ask you these things only to see what your Akash is up to. We have said there was something called the target Human.

Todd: *In this moment, the key attribute is a magnetic driver with a particular geometry both above and below the so-called target Human. So there were both magnetics — there was the no-zone point that creates the entanglement and there was the importance of a counter rotation and counter spin.*

Very good! Impressive. Now, the big question. So the Human is entangled, is it? With what is the Human quantumly entangled with? Do you remember? Let me ask you this. How many Humans are in the room?

Todd: *About 10.*

Indeed. And is there a special one?

Todd: *The template Human.*

Correct! Ah, indeed. Do you remember any other attribute about the template Human that would be noticeable if you saw him/her? You're not there yet. And that is what we're going to jog in your memory today, if it's all right with you.

Todd: *Sure.*

I'll get back to you Yawee, but for now I have to go through a process for all of you to understand what is happening. In the process, there is revelation. I now take you to basic atomic structure. I've done this before, but I've never taken you to this stage. I want you to look at an electron with me, as though you are there and as small as it is. Now go slowly, my partner, for you've had no training in this and it's important that you get the message as presented and don't enhance it [Kryon speaking to Lee].

Physicists say that electrons spin. They don't, and they can't. There's no surface on an electron, since they are energy. They don't spin, but instead have an electric potential. Every single particle on this planet, everything you can see, all things in this Universe, are created with polarity. This is new information now. All things are created with polarity, and they're designed to be self-balancing. And because of the polarity of what you would call plus and minus, they move and try to balance themselves within a field – all things, both physical and other.

However, all polarities are prone to be biased by what I will call *peer pressure*. Electrons that carry (or *spin* with a polarity) of what you would call a certain kind of charge – we'll call it positive – are drawn to those that are negative so that they will null themselves out. They seek each other out to create the null of balance. They seek to be balanced, and if they are not, they are not *happy*. I use this word only to emphasize the condition of a particle of physics that does not find its balance. Even the unscientific can appreciate this.

But even with atoms, there are not always matched pairs of electrons, since there is no atomic rule that says that electrons will always be created in even numbers. So there will often be what I will call the *odd one out* and when that happens, the entire atom will then be charged positively or negatively, depending upon the odd one out. When this happens, this atom will seek out another atom, which has an odd one out of the opposite charge. That has a name: Magnetism. I've just explained magnetism. Now, science knows part of that already. What they have not realized yet, however, is that all things have a duality. They suspect it and there are theories that will show it soon enough, and I've given it to you today because it always has existed in someone's mind.

So from the very smallest to the very biggest, even the galaxy has duality. At the center of your galaxy, what you call the black hole, is a quantum push/pull engine, and I'm going to tell you in a minute why it's that way.

Here is a big question, and I will answer it right now. Why does everything have a polarity? Why would it be created this way, even down to the electron? The smallest thing, even to what you call the Higgs Boson [God Particle] and the quarks, all have polarity. There isn't a piece of nature that you're going to find that doesn't have polarity. Why? I will tell you why: Physicists will laugh. Not in ridicule, but in agreement. If it were not this way, the Universe would be a dull, boring place to be. Because, by creating a duality in every single particle, you create an active Universe that is self-balancing and is never at rest. If it were not this way, it would be static, unchanging, and non-creative. Therefore, without polarity, there would be no life. Life is created by having a duality, a polarity in atomic particles. Life is that which is necessary for the Universe to exist. There's no reason for physics without life – and you thought it was the other way around, didn't you? Life was an accident on one planet. Oh, how 3D of you! Life *is* the DESIGN.

Let's continue the discussion, for it's going someplace. Yawee, you just described the process of creating macro-entanglement in the Temple. What you described was magnetics and null points. Very good! Do you perhaps understand that magnetics and null points are even at the center of your galaxy?

Todd: *Of course.*

So that means the galaxy is in an entangled state with itself. This now explains why all the constellations and solar systems are not following Newtonian movement. Instead, they all move at the same speed as one around the center, because they are entangled. I've just given the reason for it, and science will start to understand that soon. It has been a mystery so far, but now you know.

So you have macro-entanglement. The largest thing you can imagine, the galaxy, is entangled with itself. Is it possible there are other entanglement issues that you don't see or recognize or know about in every single day of life? And the answer's yes. So here we go.

Oh, dear Human Being, what I'm going to give you next is beautiful, and it has to do with DNA and Yawee knew it. He knew how to do something magical.

The blueprint for DNA is perfect. The good doctor will tell you that in his current incarnation [as Todd]. I've told you that before. It's perfect inside you, yet you sit here with DNA that doesn't work well. It seems to be a dichotomy, since it is perfect and designed for extended life, yet it does some things that contradict that.

DNA is designed as an informational source to receive the energy of that which is around it, created by the consciousness of humanity. It then postures itself in an appropriate reaction to the energy it is in. In other words, if the planet has low energy, it will, too. It's a quantum engine, and if the quantum energy created by Human consciousness is low, it works poorly.

I want to define life for you – not biological life, but *spiritual life*. So for all those intellectuals, just hold on, for many won't like this. Spiritual life, as measured by Spirit, is when a Human has free choice. When is that? It's when they take their first breath. Not in utero. There will be those who will say, *"That's wrong, that's wrong. The soul in the woman's body is alive!"* Just wait. I'm talking about spiritually -that which Spirit sees when you come from the other side of the veil and take your first breath.

A child with the mother has no free choice. That child is linked to the choice of the mother until it is born. It is, indeed, a soul in preparation for free choice, and there are many attributes that are spiritual that we have discussed before about how that soul reacts. But now I'm discussing life with polarity [duality], free choice.

Let's discuss that "child inside" for a moment, for there is a process I want you to know about. I want to talk about 240 days into the pregnancy. At about that time, the child has *perfect DNA*.

It hasn't taken its first breath. The DNA hasn't measured the energy of the planet yet, since it is contained. Did you realize that? Inside the womb is a perfect child. The child's DNA has all the attributes of the Akash and also the parent, but it's different in a way you have not been told. The DNA is 100% as designed.

The quantum instructions within the DNA are all talking to the biology of the child, getting ready for the first breath. Now, I reveal to you, Todd, Yawee, what you already know.

Explanation of the Temple of Rejuvenation

The Temple of Rejuvenation has two Human Beings quantumly entangled. One is the target. The other one is the "template." Life extension, through the knowledge of DNA that Yawee had, was to entangle the target with the template and transfer certain attributes from the one to the other.

The only way this could ever work is if DNA had a quantum attribute, and it does. All our teaching for more than 10 years has told you that the 90 percent of DNA that is non-encoded and considered "junk" is a quantum instruction set. Therefore, the DNA molecule must have some quantum attributes yet to be discovered, but that are very real and have to do with instructions to the chemistry of more than three billion parts of the DNA molecule. This is especially true to the gene-producing chemistry of the protein-encoded parts. For simplicity, I tell you that DNA is actively dynamic and can change the reality of everything you think of as "normal."

Yawee, you explained very well the attributes of the target creating an entangled state with the template Human. Now we reveal that the template was (1) a woman (2) who is pregnant. You have...

Todd interrupting: ... *the source of the perfect DNA template!*

That is correct! So the secret of the Temple of Rejuvenation is twofold: (1) DNA is perfect on Earth within an unborn child, and you can transfer some of the attributes of that perfection before it assimilates the energy of the planet. (2) You can extend life and healing through quantum communication with the DNA molecule. Do you see the implications? The wise, divine feminine who is with child is the only one who could be on the template table. Are you starting to understand the beauty of this, the implications of this and where it's going?

There are several things that are going to happen in mainstream science. First, you're going to find some secrets of DNA and they're going to be embryonic. Start watching scientists discover the embryonic cells and the magic within them. You already know that unusual stem cells exist in the placenta. You also know that the pre-programmed adult stem cells are still there in the body. But what about the DNA of the unborn? (Intellectuals, please keep reading, for to stop now will create unrest.) Second, your work today, Yawee, will represent "the perfect template" without using what you did in Lemuria. That's why you're the Human who will do this. It's an extension of why you came here, and is perfect for 2012 and beyond.

These embryonic cells of the unborn are untouchable by society, and they might as well be on Mars, for no science is going to try to use these cells in a 3D manner, which is all you know how to do at this point. If they try, it won't work anyway. There are quantum processes you are learning about that are not only non-invasive, but actually helpful, and that can transfer attributes from one biological cell to another and from one Human to another. Think "wireless" [Kryon humor again]. What you thought would take wires over 1,000 miles long is now done with satellites. It's an analogy that shows you that you are moving into totally new understandings of the transfer of energy. Let's discuss the mother in that temple for a moment.

The woman on the table back then, who is the "template," won the "Lemurian lottery" [Kryon being funny], for she knows that her baby, being entangled with another Human no matter how old or how sick, creates an enhancement of who that baby will be. This is complicated, but the process of helping the other will be etched into the baby's Akash, and the child will be born with an attribute of the healer. There is complexity and controversy and over-intellectual thinking in all this, for your 3D brains will race to find things wrong with it. All I can tell you is that a quantum system is not a linear one, and your logic will fall on the floor if you try to analyze these things. Can you imagine time in a circle? Can you see being in two places at the same time, or even changing your molecular structure at will to be part of another object? If you can't do that, then you are not allowed to comment reasonably. For all those things are part of the quantum possibilities of DNA. If you don't believe me, ask a Pleiadian [more cryptic Kryon humor].

Now, Yawee, are you understanding what you were doing back then? Do you need any more answers?

Todd: *Well, I could say, do I? Yes!*

[Laughter]

Yawee, what is it that you dream about? What is it that you dream about that you don't know and want to?

Todd: *I dream about recalibration of the DNA and the coherent alignment that allows us to move freely, I guess, as the Pleiadians do in a quantum state from one place to another.*

Of course you would ask that, since you see a much larger picture based on what your Akash has seen and remembers. You also know it's possible.

Meanwhile, all those in here are asking the same thing about what they just heard: *"Where can we find a pregnant woman and do this now?"*

[Laughter]

It's way beyond that, and the Pleiadians knew it. All this information originally came from them and passed to you, Yawee. It was for then, not now. The Pleiadians don't need a pregnant woman in order for them to do what they do today. They have DNA, too, but it's in a fully developed quantum state – a state that is the potential for the Human race.

I would remind you that my partner has given you messages in the past about the *attitude* of physics. Now we are right back to the polarity discussion that started this channelling. This "attitude," Yawee, is imbued into the natural invention that you have discovered. Physics is active and seeks balance. That is to say that every field you have created with your process has the attributes – are you ready? – of perfect DNA. It already sees the attributes of the blueprint of the unborn. You don't need a pregnant woman. The attributes can be passed to the Human and received by that Human in whatever posture that his cellular structure is able to absorb.

What you have done in your work is to create a quantum field with those Pleiadian attributes, and the cells *listen* when they are exposed to them. It's not finely tuned yet, but you will discover how eventually. When you do, you will have the regeneration engine of the future, without a "template Human," but instead with the attributes of the template Human.

This process and others will be seen by science also. You won't be alone. It is not appropriate that you would have the secret of life exclusively, so there will be others. Embryonic studies with animals are going to start to reveal that which gives Humans the ability to grow back limbs and many of the other things we have talked about for 23 years. It begs a still greater question: "What is the true role of animals on the planet? Do they reincarnate?" This is for another time.

Look for these kinds of things to happen soon, and also the use of adult stem cells in a bigger way. And there it is, all laid out in front of you. All of this has been waiting for 2012.

Yawee, one of your attributes is that you *live* with the Pleiadians. You are still in an entangled state with them, which is not in 3D. They want to hear the tones again as they did 26,000 years ago. They're ready. And when that signal is sent, it will say *"humanity has arrived and is going to stay"* [speaking of Todd's Lemurian Choir Project for the solstice of 2012].

And that is the message for the day. Some will say, *"Too much science, Kryon!"* Others will say, *"Indeed, the beauty of the system of the Creator is at hand."* Dear ones, don't be turned away with the particulars of the science. You don't have to know and understand it, but we ask you to celebrate it. For God the Creator is the master physicist of the Universe and has used these tools to create the system of life and the balance of love. All of this is going to enhance Human life and Human understanding.

Again, I will tell you that the distance between the nucleus and the electron of every single atom is filled with the love of God. That's the soup of the Creator, built for life and ready to take your hand if you want it to. It is the recalibration of knowledge on the planet and the first step into a quantum paradigm. Get ready for it.

I have no clock. I can't tell you when. I can only tell you that it is at hand and it was not when we started with you all those years ago. We passed the marker together and now the work begins.

And so it is.

For all those who have asked...

One of the hardest questions to answer for me is, *"What is it like while you are in the chair?"* The real answer is, you wouldn't believe it if I told you. That has been the standard answer. It was just too personal and way too hard to talk (or write) about. So now I will. It's time to let a total stream of consciousness take over and let you know. Please, this isn't casual reading. Get ready.

Lee Carroll

Chapter Three
THE CHANNELLING EXPERIENCE

Kryon
Book 13

Chapter Three
The Channelling Experience
Lee Carroll

I sit in the chair and it's silent. It doesn't matter the number of people in the audience before me. I've done this in auditoriums filled with people and also in the wilderness within a circle of only a few. The feeling is that I'm about to cross the bridge, and there is always hesitation.

I'm about to step into a mist of a reality that cannot be described. Oh, you can learn to channel, but nobody can teach you what I'm about to feel and see. The mist is where the love is, and it's a place where you want to stay. The 3D mind is not prepared, and it took me over a decade to go to this purity, to this place, where I'm suspended between what I know in 3D and what I "know" as a child of God.

How do I explain the dimensional shift of every cell being whispered to? While I'm in channel, my cellular structure changes – oh, that feeling! I keep my eyes shut, but suddenly I don't have eyes. Others can channel with their eyes open. I can't.

Spirit has removed the filters of 3D and has taken me out of my reality, but I'm still in my body. Nobody can teach this. There is no way to teach how to become pure and leave everything you have learned behind. You can't teach how to look back and only see one side of duality. You have left the shore and are looking back at the very essence of humanism, which you no longer are involved with.

Reader, sense quietness as you read this.

There is no sound where I am. There is the feeling of a breeze of some sort, a whispering wind. It has a message I can't decipher, and yet I can. It's a familiar voice in a language I know so well, but can't quite remember. I'm not channelling yet, or am I? There is no reference of time, and I feel the grandness of something more. What is it? What part of me am I about to meet?

"Who is there?"

The message to my cells is being delivered all at once and not through sound. Am I speaking in the chair yet? Does it matter? Will I return to my reality? Does it matter? Suddenly, I hear a voice and it's disconnected, but it's the voice of Lee. It sounds odd, since it's only one of many I have in me. My Akash rings with the truth of what is happening and the whispering voice grows louder.

"Greetings, dear ones, I am Kryon of Magnetic Service."

Could it be I'm just beginning? I've been in the mist for a long time! I know where I am! I've been here before, many times. Should I be afraid? This is the path we all eventually take to the light!

Many have come to this place on their way to another. I know that. When we take our last breath, it's where we go. We have a suspension of all that is real or ever has been real, and the whispering wind begins to guide us along a path to the light. But in my case, there is no path, for I have agreed to step in and out. But, indeed, there is a kind of path, one where I pause and wait.

I can feel humanity in front of me in the room, but I feel their Akash and not their physical bodies. Lee is speaking. I'm listening and remembering, which is my agreement with Kryon. I'm not somewhere else. I'm here with Lee. But oh, that whispering voice! I don't want to leave, ever.

Many have come to this place on their way to another. Some deny this reality. Some feel they are dead. Some are frightened, but most are very peaceful. The path only goes one way, and the breeze blows toward the light. Some go to the brink of the light and return. But once you hear the voice of that wind, you are never the same.

What happens to Humans who are taken on a trip where the reality of where they are is stronger than the reality of being a Human as they know it? How can that be? The answer is that they long for the "real" place even after they have come back into their bodies. Nobody can talk you out of it, for you experienced it and know that it's "out there". You have felt the reality of your place in the Universe and Human life becomes just a detour.

I have touched the face of the wind for years, but only in the last four years has Kryon allowed me to stay in it, feel it, listen to it, and be consumed by it. The mist deepens, but I'm not afraid of it. I've practiced this for two decades and now I know that I can go back. There is never fear. Never. Lee continues to speak, and somehow I continue to be cognizant of all of it.

The message being given to the Humans is a very elementary one. It's the 3D ABCs of a quantum alphabet, which is infinite. How can I describe this? The language turns into something more. It feels like the very breath of God, my sustenance and strength, the core of everything that is. I want to stay here. All is well here.

Kryon knows when to stop. Many can channel for hours, but I cannot. Most Kryon channels are under an hour, and sometimes much less. Why? It's the limit of my ability to stay in the wind without surrendering to the whispers that tell me I'm "Home".

My ancestors are here. The longer I stay, the more the mist clears. I can see who I am and who I've been. My DNA is expanding to let me "see" the grandness of my journey. Those who planted the seeds within mc are starting to appear.

Lee is still speaking, but now it doesn't matter. The whispering voice is starting to become music. Oh please, let me hear and identify this song. I know this song! I'm on another planet, but I'm not. I'm everywhere, but I'm not. The song is beyond beautiful. It is Home. There is splendor here.

Cellular division has stopped. Aging has stopped. Who knows what else has stopped? Who cares? I'm on the bridge, but I still have my tether. I feel it tugging on me and the silver glow of it pulls on my heart. Why must I return? When I'm Home, why must I return? How much longer is the tether going to keep me as a Human?

The music grows slightly louder and I'm just beginning to "hear" what it could be. How can light be music? How can I hear light? Oh my!

"And so it is."

I'm back. I'm in the chair. It's over, and there is often sadness that I can't show anyone.

Many need to read this. Someday, my dear friends, we will all walk that path again. I will do it, too, for the final time as Lee. When that happens and the tether is released, I will hear that music and "remember" everything. I will hear the voice in the wind and know the song. Then I will be Home.

At death, the quantum parts of our DNA expand to touch the face of God. Parts of it go back to the Cave of Creation and parts go to the creative source itself. Our soul is alive, more alive than ever, and free of the bounds of the frailness of the body we carried around for all those years. There are release and joy. There are understanding and infinite wisdom. All of us will take our turn, for it's the way of things – all of us. How do I know? Because I go there often, and I've seen it and felt it. Kryon allows me to sit and watch and "know".

Meanwhile, those left behind to mourn are consumed with grief, for in their world all they see is loss and sorrow and loneliness. If only they would call on their own Akash to remember – remember.

Death has no sting. Even the very word is clinical, for at the soul level there is only transition, and the transition called "death" is glorious! Life is only as we define it, but the truth is that we all live forever.

Many times, my seminars finish after a Kryon channelling. In the small groups, I often ask that they dismiss themselves and stay and meditate if they wish. This allows me to "come down" from the mountain (as they say) and recalibrate.

In the larger, team-based seminars, I often remove myself from the stage long before those of my staff do. Often, Peggy Phoenix Dubro, Robert Coxon, and Dr. Todd Ovokaitys stay. They dance, greet, and have another 10 minutes or so of goodbye time. I'm not able to do this. I'm still hearing the wind and trying to sort out what my reality is. This is the first time I have admitted this anywhere. If you have witnessed this through the years, now you know the whole story. So when you see me leave the stage quickly, now you know why.

Lee Carroll

It's time to Get Big!

Still in January, we now find ourselves on a cruise ship in Patagonia. This is the southernmost tip of South America, and Kryon lets us know how the very solar system and time itself will be recalibrating.

Lee Carroll

Chapter Four
THE RECALIBRATION OF THE UNIVERSE
Patagonia
January 2012
Kryon
Book 13

Chapter Four
The Recalibration of The Universe
Live Kryon Channelling - January 2012

Greetings, dear ones, I am Kryon of Magnetic Service. There is so much I want to tell you, but again, we start softly. We honor the energy in the room. We create a bubble of wisdom around us, so those who wish to hear will do so. We speak to many, not just those in the room. I want you to honor this moment, for it's for you. This is not idle information. This information has a profound, Human stamp on it. It means that whatever I'm telling you, you have created. I'm aware that this message is being given in two languages [Spanish and English]. The information is complex, yet simple. We need you to listen to understand concepts prepared in advance for you by those on this side of the veil who know who you are.

There is a shift going on in this planet. If you are indeed an old soul, it is affecting you, and each of you has a different affectation. That is to say, each one of you will have a different way of responding to the energy. Old souls have something very interesting. They may be old souls, but that means that each of them has a vastly different experience of lives. So each of you is going to react separately and uniquely to the energy of the planet's shift. However, all of you are feeling something interesting. It's an enhancement of your wisdom and knowledge, and the feeling that the energy on the planet is moving in a direction that is toward your consciousness and not away from it.

We've talked about how Humans are recalibrating, and now there's one that you didn't expect – how the Universe is recalibrating. It's a difficult premise that I bring forward to you today, for it has concepts outside of three dimensions. And so I will go slowly.

Time

We start with the very predictions of the energy you are in. Let us say that you have a racetrack with cars on it. Picture a track that is very large – really large. Let us say that it takes years for the drivers to race around the track. They get tired. Sometimes they will get out of the car and put a new driver in. Sometimes the new driver will get tired and the older driver will come back and get in again. So some of the race cars are filled with experienced drivers and some are not. It might take them years to go around the track just one time.

Let us say that there is a difficult portion of the track, one that is filled with holes. Some don't see them and the newest drivers fall into the holes. The older drivers know to go around. Now in your three-dimensional perception, it is not difficult for you to imagine such a thing. But this is a metaphor of time.

The track represents your 3D concept of time, which you think it is a straight road. It is not. It is a circle. Now pretend for a moment you're one of the drivers in one of the cars, unaware of the circle. Also, let us say that you've been around the track many times. The new driver may think the track is straight and unending, for it disappears into the horizon. But as the old soul, you know that the track is really huge and the curve just can't be seen, much like the curvature of the earth. So as an old soul driver, you know where the difficult places in the track are. You also realize in this metaphor that as you drive forward and look out the front of your car, you are looking at a future and the past at the same time. This is one of the premises that a three-dimensional mind cannot grasp – that as you change the future, you are also driving over and changing the past. That premise alone explains how the predictions for 2012 can happen at all.

But 2012 is simply one of the difficult places in the track, and the Ancients knew it was coming. They could prophesy a problem ahead on the track because it's part of the circle. It's well known in time, and those who might give a name to it would call it *fractal time*. In past Human history, some of the difficult parts actually created the termination of humanity. Some have resulted in a start-over of humanity. The energy that you are in now had a duality in its potential. You could have started over or you could start something the planet had never seen before.

Twenty-two years ago, we told you this: "Get ready for a shift," we said. "Get ready for the weather to change," we said. Those things have now come about. They came about not because Kryon or the prophets said they would, but because of old souls who saw the difficulty coming. They had gone around the circle of time before and knew where the issues were. It was "known" territory.

The most difficult thing I can tell you for you to conceive of this is: As you steer around these difficulties and move forward on the track, you change the energy of the entire track. Therefore, you change the past as you move toward the future. This is not an easy concept to understand; however, it explains so much to the linear mind of how these things can be. For in your 3D perception, you believe that your experience in the future is going to be a product of what took place in the past. You only go in one direction and your expectations are in a straight line. All you have is your experience in the past – and it's not good enough.

As you change the track, you change the rules of the track. So what I wish to say that is simplified is that there is a new paradigm ahead of you. Old souls will see it first, and they will plant the seeds for the rest of humanity. The young people will see it, for they have it in their Akashic inheritance. Slowly, Human nature itself will change and move into a new way of thinking where you're not guided only by the experience of things that took place in what you think is your past. It's an amazing potential. You are not the only planet who has experienced this. However, you are the only planet in your galaxy that is experiencing it *now*.

The Bigger Picture

Now I'm going to say things that are esoterically unbelievable. Your galaxy knows what's happening here on Earth. I'm not talking about life forms in your galaxy. I'm talking about the very physics of what you think lies there as the "rules." The Universe is cooperating with your shift – expected it – for this is why you came.

Now it gets difficult to explain. You think physics is simply the rules of the way things work? Let me ask you a question: How do you explain what some astronomers have named "intelligent design"? Against all odds, the Universe was created for life. Physics is supposed to be random, following rules that are random. Yet it didn't happen that way. The better the instruments of the astronomer became, the more they realized there had to be intelligence in the design. How do you explain that? All they know is the math. What you see before you, which you call your galaxy, is equivalent to rolling a six on the dice 10,000 times in a row! And it makes no sense, since it isn't random and it doesn't follow the bell-shaped curve of nature. That is why they are saying what they are saying.

There had to be a guiding force of creation. Does that change your mind about physics or about what you see before you? I will tell you how actual physics is beginning to cooperate with you. This time fractal has been known for a long time, and you could have gone many ways. In other words, you had many potentials of consciousness. Look at the prophecies of the Ancients. They said you were going to have a world war. They said you were going to have termination. Many spiritual systems called for the end of the world where your souls would be collected. Many systems would have you believe a certain way so that you would be prepared – and none of those things happened! Does that tell you a little bit about the shift before you? Different paradigms of thinking are coming. These paradigms will deal with problems you have that are currently seen as "unsolvable". So let us start with some unbelievable things.

The Magnetics of the Solar System

Now, my partner, I want you to go slow for both yourself and the translator. Twenty-two years ago, we told you the magnetic field of the earth was critical to your consciousness. Magnetics is a quantum energy. So is gravity, and so is light. You are surrounded by a quantum field that is the magnetic field of the earth. We said if Human consciousness is going to change, magnetics will change. It has to. It has to be a complement to what you are doing. It has to posture itself to receive what you are doing. How can the consciousness of this planet expand when the magnetics stay the same? It can't. So the magnetics must move.

So it started with an actual shift of the magnetic ley lines of your planet, and that's now recorded history and something I predicted more than 20 years ago. Now your compasses show you that all I spoke about is now here. Your magnetics has moved greatly since 1989.

Now, there has to be more. What else do you think could change the magnetics of your entire planet? It has to recalibrate, and in order for it to do so, it's going to need help. Your solar system is the engine of magnetic change for this planet. If you know anything about how the solar system works and the energies of it, then this will start to make sense.

In your solar system, the core is the sun. It sends out what is called the solar wind, which is almost entirely magnetic. It's a magnetic energy that literally blasts out from the sun and contains only what was generated from the sun. That magnetic energy has a name – the heliosphere. It "blows" that magnetic wind against the magnetics of your own earth, and that changes your planet.

If the energy is always the same on Earth, then very little will ever change. For those who wish to get technical, you might say the magnetics of the sun blow against the magnetics of the earth and you will have two interacting magnetic fields. This creates something called inductance, which is a mystery to science. It's the "soup" of overlapping magnetic fields that allows for the energy exchange of information and amplification without a power source. It's well used on Earth, but the attributes are seen as mysterious.

So here's what's going to happen. Watch for changes in your sun. You may call them solar storms, but they're just a recalibration for you, and they will worry you. This is because there are many sensitive electronics on and around the planet, and these instruments will react. You count on the magnetic field of your planet to remain the same, but it can't remain the same when there is a giant solar storm happening. Certain kinds of communications will be disrupted. Perhaps even the power grid could be interrupted.

Watch the sun, for it is in the process of shift. It is happening through intelligent design, the love of God and the Creator, changing things for your consciousness. It is a new way of thinking that is developing, literally touching the very DNA field of each Human. This changes the information within the DNA and allows the Human Being to capture and enhance attributes of a new reality it never had before.

Now I get even more physical: Something has been *on the way* for a very long time. The magnetics of your solar system itself are changing. So here's the challenge: Go find that fact. You'll see it, literally, as your solar system moves through space. It intersects certain attributes of space, and this is changing some of the magnetics, which then become different from the way they ever were before. This then changes the sun. Do you see the cycle? One enhances the other in a fractal of circular reality. Your movement around the center changes your solar system. The solar system's new position changes the sun's attributes. The sun's attributes are sent to the planet via the heliosphere and this affects your DNA.

Now, the intellectuals will say, *"Well, this does not make sense. Those processes ready to impact the earth have been on the way for eons, ready to intersect your solar system – so they haven't 'just happened.' In other words, this would have happened no matter what. It didn't matter if you were in a consciousness shift or not."*

I accept this argument, but with explanation. Let us say in the 1600s, there was a spaceship that came by the planet broadcasting music, sending a radio transmission of music to the planet. Now let me ask you this: Was the transmission real? Yes, I just told you it was. Was the music beautiful and real? Yes. Had the spaceship been on its way for a long time? Yes. How many people on the planet heard the music? And the answer is: None of them! This is because the radio receiver had not been invented yet.

In this example, the spaceship had always been on its way. Do you see the metaphor? The magnetic changes would have happened anyway, but if the earth had not been ready, then no person would have heard any music. There would be no reaction, and Humans would be the same as they always have been, if there were even any Humans at all – for some say that you were on your way to destroying yourselves yet again.

You are changing the past by changing the future. You are rearranging the energy of your solar system and also something else. This is hard for you to conceive, dear ones, but we give it to you anyway: Very, very far away from you, things are changing. You don't believe it because they're too far away for you to consider, and in three dimensions, things that are far away are not part of your bubble of reality. However, they're in a quantum state with you.

The entire galaxy revolves as one plate, in a very counterintuitive way. The stars and the constellations do not orbit within the rules of Newtonian physics that you are used to seeing all around you in your own solar system – for distance from the center does not matter. All the stars rotate at the same speed. This is because the galaxy is entangled with the middle of itself. In that state, there is no time or distance. The change of consciousness on this planet has changed the center of the galaxy. This is because what happens here, dear one, is "known" by the center.

It's interesting to us what your scientific reaction to all this is. You saw that the "creative event" of your Universe is missing some energy in order for it to have formed as it did. In addition, the unusual way the galaxy rotates, as I just stated, was also noted. So you have calculated that for all this to be in place, there has to be missing 3D matter, and you have given it a name – "dark matter". How funny! Did you ever think that there could be a multi-dimensional effect going on that you now can observe and calculate, that has immense power, but can't be seen? It's not "matter" at all and it's not 3D. It's quantum energy.

Let me tell you something about physics. Yet again, I'll make it simple. Everything your scientists have seen in physics happens in pairs. At the moment, there are four laws of physics in your three-dimensional paradigm. They represent two pairs of energy types. Eventually, there will be six. At the center of your galaxy is what you call a black hole, but it is not a single thing. It is a duality. There is no such thing as "singularity". You might say it's one energy with two parts – a weak and a strong quantum force. And the strangest thing is, it knows who you are. It is the creator engine. It's different in other galaxies than this one. It's unique.

The very physics of your galaxy is postured by what you do here. The astronomers can look into the cosmos and they will discover different physics in different galaxies. Could it be that there's something going on in the other galaxies like this one? I'm not going to answer that.

Different Thinking

Dear Human Being, this is bigger than you think. Old soul, this is bigger than you think. This is why we plead for you to stay on this planet and to change your cellular structure, to mine your Akash and start looking inside. In other words, do not take the past and project it to your future reality, for you are able to do things now that you were never able to do before. Gaia is cooperating. The Universe is cooperating, and Lightworkers are moving into a manifestation paradigm.

Personally for your own body, many of you are getting younger instead of older. You are creating solutions to problems you thought were unsolvable. You were told today that your population is expanding at a rate of at least a billion souls every decade. So what does your past tell you the problem will be? It will be the global explosion of humanity. The result, you feel, will be lack of food and water, overcrowding and starvation. That is what your past tells you will happen.

Let me tell you what the assumption is, dear Human Being. The assumption to create this conclusion is that Human Beings are simply too dense to notice it and have no idea what to do to change it. That's the old perception, based on an old Human nature. Watch what happens. Watch…what…happens. You're going to figure it out and there will be elegant solutions to the unsolvable problems of the past.

In almost every field of science, this is coming. It will help Human Beings live longer and healthier without war. There'll come a time when there won't even be terrorism, dear ones. Oh, there will be unbalance, Human Being. That comes with life. But not country against country, not spiritual group against spiritual group.

This is what you are planting seeds for now, and the Universe knows who you are. Your galaxy resounds with your victory! Death has no sting. I will tell you this: You're all involved to come here for eons. Old souls are starting to manifest the new reality. I have no clock. I cannot tell you how long this is going to take. But you've had 18 earth years to make a big difference, for that is the energy we see.

Recalibration of Systems and New Sight

By the way, what happens to the solar system when the magnetics shift? Now you start to see where astrology will begin to shift as well. There are those who will start to apply the quantum filter to astrology. It's happening now. What is your quantum sign? It's different from the three-dimensional sign. Oh, there'll come a day, dear ones, in science, where the scientists will be able to apply what I will call a quantum filter to alter what they see. This will be a filter developed for telescopes that involves a super-cooling of the filter itself. Astronomers will be able to look out into the cosmos and, for the first time, see quantum attributes.

The first thing they'll notice is two things in the center of the galaxy, not one. The next thing will be the colors around the Human Being. And science will start a whole new section called "The Study of the Human Auric Energy." All of these are coming.

How long will all this take? That is up to you. Meanwhile, plant the seeds of understanding, of peacefulness, of appreciation and of love. Become slow to anger, slow to create drama. Take on the attributes of the masters, and that is what your abilities are changing to right now. Soften in all things. Look at each other differently.

There'll come a time when there's no war. Those in this room and those listening will know I'm right. Watch for these things in your science. When they happen, remember this day when I told you how it really works.

Blessed is the Human Being who has understood this message as personal for themselves, not about the cosmos. It's about the inner being and the journey of the soul – and the Universe within.

And so it is.

Kryon

Heavy Subjects!

In this discussion, Kryon speaks of the very essence of what we have gotten used to must change. Dark and light are absolute – or are they? What can we expect from governments for the economy? What does that have to do with the dark/light balance on the planet? Everything! Will you believe the predictions? The nice thing here is that there are those reading in the future who are laughing at how much of this has already happened!

Lee Carroll

Chapter Five
THE RECALIBRATION OF DARK AND LIGHT
San Antonio, Texas
Frebruary 2012
Kryon
Book 13

Chapter Five
The Recalibration of Dark and Light
Live Kryon Channelling - February 2012

Greetings, dear ones, I am Kryon of Magnetic Service. I speak to those who have an elegance of wisdom. You may not think of this as you, for there are those here who are literally only feeling this for the first time, but there's an elegance in this room. The elegance of discernment is here, and this is placed upon you so that you would discern what is true and what is not – including this very message.

There is a dispensation of wisdom occurring on this planet. For all those who would question themselves or what has happened this day [The Kryon Seminar] or wonder if they were manipulated with knowledge or energy, they should go inside and feel that raw, pure energy of the love of God. Raw, in that it is not clouded with a filter; you can see it for what it is. The appropriateness of all things reveals itself, including your place on the earth, living the way you're living with those you live with, with everything you've learned. Your wisdom will tell you that it is all correct and proper, and you haven't made any mistakes. You are wiser than you think.

The room is filled with old souls, and old souls make a difference on this planet. They carry energetic weight with their wisdom. You are those old souls, dear Humans. But do not put a time on this change, for neither Spirit nor Gaia will react to your clock. Instead, put the compassion of God on the change. See that which is appropriate for your life for now, and then stand back and create it. Listen to it. See it happening. Take a trip to the future where it is happening. Feel it upon your lives.

Blessed is the Human Being who knows they are a part of the plan and the system, for these are the Humans who will plant the seeds for peace on Earth.

The Energy of Recalibration

We wish to continue the series that we are calling, "The Recalibration of All Things". We have given you information in the past about the recalibration of the planet, of humanity and even of the Universe. Now we speak of the recalibration of dark and light and what it means to you.

So before I begin, I must define what I mean by dark and light and then I will also define what I mean by the new 2012 energy. When I speak about dark and light to you, what do you think about? I'll tell you what many are trained to think about: They're trained to think about evil and good and bad. They're trying to put these things in the appropriate boxes where they were taught they belong using linear thinking. They will turn to the mythology that taught them about an entity with a tail trying to capture their soul and other mysterious entities around that work for that main evil entity.

So I will tell you again: The entity that is after your soul is mythology, dear ones. It doesn't exist in your reality. But you might say, *"Wait a minute, Kryon. Are you telling me evil doesn't exist?"* No, dear ones, I didn't say that. What I'm telling you is that all the darkness on this planet has come from Human Beings. You don't need to assign energy to a mythological creature to have evil on the earth. The darkest of the dark can be created by the Humans if they choose to do that. Dark power can be created because Humans are powerful and can manifest it. Darkness is not that hard to manifest.

However, we have told you before that the light/dark balance of the planet is what is at hand. Those who carry light in the dark room will not have darkness around them, for the definition of darkness is the *absence of light*. But if there are only a few who carry the match, there's going to be a lot of darkness. So you are subject to that, for you will walk around in whatever light balance is created by humanity.

You might call it a *system*. All of life is affected – all of it – by the light and dark balance of where humanity decides to place this balance. The definition of dark and light has to do with the Human consciousness balance, since it is the Human Being who creates dark and light for the planet. It's a concept. So this is the subject of this message: *What is the new balance of the earth energy going to mean to you, personally, today?*

Second definition: The 2012 energy is a marker, a seeming perception of a time frame that you have now passed and are well into, which gives a confluence of energy permission to change reality. The earth, being Gaia, begins to shift with you and for you, and the energy of the planet moves into areas that it never has before.

The Movement of the Kundalini on Earth

I gave a channel in the area you call Peru. We talked about the prophecy of the Ancients, which was called *the journey of the feathered serpent*. This has also been called *the centering of wisdom on the planet*. Some have called it the movement of the Kundalini. The Kundalini is an energy that is always associated with movement. It is also often associated with procreation, and the metaphor is therefore dealing with the rebirth of humanity.

Civilization itself is at stake within this movement, and you've passed the marker – an alignment that many said would never happen. This is the fifth time you've been through this opportunity and now, dear ones, you're headed for the potential of peace on Earth.

Twenty-three years ago, we told you this could happen and that the potentials were strong for it. Now, all that is around you is struggling with it, for the shift is here. I'll say this over and over: The old energy of darkness dies hard, screaming and struggling to keep what it has had, and it struggles with its own demise. So that is the energy we speak of now, and the subject is *the Human consciousness balance between dark and light*. Many have called this *duality*.

How does this new balance affect you?

Let's start with the personal, then I'll go to something bigger and then something even bigger. I'll end with a prediction we've never given before – a potential that has arisen only recently.

Dear ones, I am Kryon. I give you information of love about the planet and your own energy. I never give you information that has not already been generated by the potential of Human consciousness. Quite often the predictions are given and then they happen. When they do, you consider that fortune telling. It is not. It is energy in that random, chaotic place you called *quantum*, weighing the potentials of what could happen regarding your lives and the earth. So the future is driven by the potentials that you have created with your own consciousness as a civilization on the planet – not fortune telling, but a measurement of what you are creating.

Twenty-three years ago, we saw the potentials of today, for you were starting to develop these very things and the seeds were being planted for what you are seeing now. It's beautiful and difficult at the same time. Change is always accompanied with difficulty. Even the most well-balanced Human will say, *"I have found my balance and I'm pleased with this balance."* Then someone comes along and says, *"Well, we're going to change things."* That's when that well-balanced Human yells, *"No! I'm balanced. Don't change anything!"* For change means you're going to put a weight on one side of that balance scale and you're going to have to learn to shift so that you center again. That's always unpleasant and a lot of work. But that's not what you're going to be doing this time. This time it's even harder! We call it recalibration.

Let me tell you what it means by giving you a short review of a message [channelling] I gave recently. In an older energy, you went about protecting yourselves from darkness. If you were a healer, you *protected* yourselves from those who might have imbalance, psychological problems, even disease in their bodies. Then you often did a number of things to make sure you were protected. There was a process, a procedure for that. I'm telling you right now that this process is gone.

This is a review. If you're constantly creating light, then darkness does not have a chance. We've said this over and over and now it comes full circle to you personally: Wherever you go, darkness can't touch you. Are you listening to me? It can't touch you. The essence of your light is the love of God and you are broadcasting it, Lightworker – broadcasting it! There's no dark thing that can get in there as long as you're broadcasting light!

Now let me tell you a guaranteed way where you can *stop broadcasting light* and open yourselves up to go backwards instead of forward. It's by saying, *"I can't do it. Who am I? I'm not worthy."* There will be many spiritual leaders who will tell you you're not worthy. They will tell you that you were born dirty and unworthy to even talk to God. They will tell you that you have to suffer to get the attention and approval of God. However, God is in you, and even the master of love told you that. Therefore, you are not born dirty, but born magnificent! If God is in you, then light is in you.

We move on to point two: Drama, anger, frustration. There's a lot of it. So when you leave this room, how much of that are you going to participate in? It depends upon the duality, doesn't it? If you are a Lightworker, a lighthouse on this planet who changes the balance of light everywhere you walk, then you're going to be given immediate power over anger, frustration and drama. Power over it! Now, you can't change the people around you. You just can't. They will flail and do whatever they want to and they may go into anger and drama. They may even try to push your buttons. I think you know who I'm talking about. I know who's here and who is reading. They'll do it in order to get control over you, and if they can affect you, you've fallen for it, haven't you?

If a person can get dramatic, if they can get angry enough, if they can push your buttons, then they just won the light/dark battle. For years, this has been a struggle because the balance of dark and light has always teetered in the middle of balance, but so often favored the dark. The dark was easy and blind. During these years, the Lightworkers had to work hard to gain the upper hand for themselves, so they would not be affected by the other. I hope you understand what I'm saying. It has been an upstream swim for the Lightworker!

Now, however, energy is being delivered to you as this earth shifts, which is going to make it far easier for you, the Lightworker, to be in control of your emotions, no matter what is around you. Then you can stand there with all the angels on your side, while others try all they want to affect you, but you won't need to react. I challenge you to do this, for there'll be those of you who walk into the workplace in a couple of days and may have a challenge. It is the way of 3D. The old balance will still be there trying to assert itself in an old way, not being aware that you've changed. So what will your reaction be? Can you begin to take your power?

What happens when one person takes the high road? Eventually that road is where the other person will want to be also! It's well-lighted and attractive. You don't just change yourself by creating light. What you do on this planet is seen by all. Every single small victory at home or at work will help you walk in a peaceful way where you didn't before. That victory is seen by everybody, and you seem better balanced.

All of us on this side know what you have done! Listen to our applause when you walk from a place and know you did it: You didn't fall for it this time, and you are not affected anymore. Some of you know of what I speak. Anger, frustration, drama – they don't have to be in your life at all.

Perhaps you've decided, as you walk from place to place, that you may have to get out of town, get out of a relationship, get out of a job, for things to settle for you. Now I want you to rethink that idea for a moment. What happens if things start to change for you personally and the things that bothered you before now don't? That changes the conditions, doesn't it? Now you can be in the same situations you always were, and yet it's completely different. You're not frustrated anymore. You don't get angry anymore, even as those around you continue to spin in drama and unrest. You actually have more wisdom due to it and can manifest better.

I'll tell you what may eventually happen. Those *spinners* will see you, and eventually some are going to come to you in private and say, *"How do you do it? I wish I didn't have to spin so much. I see that you've changed. For some reason, you're not bothered anymore. For some reason, you have a smile and I can see the peace of God in you and I want it. You don't gossip. You don't make other people wrong. You honor all people when you open your mouth and speak. I can hear it. Something has changed in you and I'd love to know what it is."* Then, my dear Human Being, and only then, should you open up and say, *"I've found something that I never thought existed. I found God inside me."* That's powerful, and your actions prove it.

Number three: Are you aware of how your body is shifting? It's allowing you to not only to heal yourself, but also to feel better as you do it. This creates a cellular communication where you don't age as much. Your body will stay younger when the chemistry doesn't have to deal with anxiety.

The Planetary Balance

A summary: On this planet, the balance of what has happened, what Humans have done through the ages, stays here. It is recorded quantumly in what is called *the Crystalline Grid*. Everything that takes place on the planet, which Humans create, stays here as energy.

Every situation where energy is created stays in the Crystalline Grid. If there's a dark energy created by Humans, the Crystalline Grid emanates darkness. If there's a light energy, it emanates light.

For 23 years and the last 18 in particular, you have changed the dark/light balance of Gaia. In the process, your DNA starts to shift. *It is quantumly tuned to the Crystalline Grid.* That is to say, it then starts to shift not only in you, but also in every baby that's born. You might say that the Human DNA field "looks around" at birth and picks up the energy that is given to it by the Crystalline Grid. That, then, is the starting energy it will have for life. Therefore, what you do now affects the energy of the earth and even the consciousness of humanity to come. Think about it. For eons, nothing has changed. Human nature was always the same and, therefore, you never saw anything but war and frustration. This is now starting to change, and the Lightworkers on the planet have created it.

The children are changing. They're different. Some of them are taking on quantum attributes. Many adults laugh at this concept, as they sit and enjoy a better earth, not even acknowledging the considerable change before them, since they are in their own box of reality. But that's what's going on, and it's because the dark and light balance of the earth is affecting newborn DNA. History is not repeating itself, and instead of the planet's population continuing to separate and split itself apart, it is attempting slowly to put itself together. This will happen over generations, so it's not as obvious as something that happens on a week to week basis, which Humans would rather look at in their impatience and intellectual pursuit of a fast-moving reality.

What this means is that you can stay here longer, no matter what you've been told. Longer life is in your grasp – a lot longer. I'm talking to somebody who needed to hear that. We've given instructions on creating pure intent. We've told you that if you start a process of belief, where you literally go inside and become *one with that which is your innate self* [innate is the quantum intelligence of biology], then you are beginning to move into a more multi-dimensional Human, the true reality of all the matter in the Universe. Being 3D is not a normal reality. It's the reality of a closed system of thinking and begets only what it knows instead of moving into what it can imagine.

Innate intelligence? Why would you use kinesiology unless you wanted to know something you don't know? Innate is the energy that you contact when you do muscle testing. Innate is the key. The dark and light balance of the planet is starting to move into a lighter balance, and then it becomes easier for you to contact your own cellular structure and start a process that will operate by itself, as long as you continue to desire light in your life.

Stop Assigning Power to an Outside Force

It's time for you to stop giving credit to the almighty *outside* and give credit to the almighty *inside*, as the masters did. What if the true divinity and power on the planet are hidden in Human Beings instead of angels in the sky or big buildings with impressive facades? Humans love to give away their power to others, both Human and not, since most Humans don't trust themselves. But what if balanced health could be yours and you could stop the aging process? Dear ones, you should live 200 years, at least! You rejuvenate! This is your design, but this design is not operating at full efficiency due to the dark/light balance that has been on the planet for eons. Now it is changing.

You're going to start seeing something in the next generation and the one after that: extended life without science. It's going to start happening automatically, and it will be a puzzle for the biologists. Why would Humans start living so much longer? They will say, *"Maybe it's nutrition. Maybe it's this and maybe it's that. Maybe it's the lack of disease because we're curing them."* They'll have all number of reasons and none of them will be accurate, because they don't know the energy of what you've done and how it's affecting the DNA. Counter-intuitive to all the pollution you are pumping into the environment, Humans will start to have extended lifetimes.

Governments

Let me talk about governments, because you're going to see some change. First, look at history: For years, even in your lifetime and those of your grandparents, the leadership of countries has decided to conquer one another simply because they could! There was an unspoken barbaric attitude that, *"If we are more powerful, then we deserve to conquer the weak and take their land."* This is history and wasn't all that long ago.

Let me remind you, 30,000 years of your past history is filled with this. It's literally *the history of humanity.* Whoever had the most power invaded the one who did not, did you notice? The strong one didn't have to have a reason, either. If a country had no army, then they eventually had no country! Today, that is no longer in your consciousness, or that of most current governments. But sometimes it still happens, and when you see it, even on a small scale, it disgusts you, does it not? That entire attitude doesn't seem to be valid anymore, and it's shocking when you see it. There's now more respect for sovereignty and the idea of conquering is something from the past.

Governments change. Attitudes change. So you might say, *"Well, we licked that one. We've gone someplace."* And you'd be right, for the planet really has changed in that regard. So, what about the next one? What is next for government that is vastly different from the "norm" that you grew up in? You're going to start seeing a change in the way government conducts itself. Believe it or not, you're going to start seeing more integrity! There will be those who demand it and those who will shrink from it and this is where the battles will be.

You may even see in your lifetime the end to name-calling during elections! Now, wouldn't that be something, where one candidate stands up and says, *"I don't agree with my opponent, but he's a patriot and I can see that he loves his country as I do. I don't agree with him, and here is why and what I stand for."* This is more than taking the high road. It's a new paradigm of thinking.

Right now, you are more prone to say, *"My opponent is a bad guy. Look at what he's done and look at the mistakes he's made and look at his personal ways of dishonesty and mischief."* That's an old paradigm, dear ones. I want you to watch for this change. The first one who does it on a major political stage will create a breath of fresh air in your politics, and the system will never be the same. The new paradigm will be seen as viable by those who study these things. When you start seeing it in that arena, you'll know it's real. You're headed for an election year [this channelling was in February 2012]. Don't expect much change, because the old energy is strong. It may take four more years for you to see a difference, perhaps even four more after that. But someone will come along who sets a standard that will be so different that everyone will know it's something that really works.

When the Indigos run for office, there will be a shift in the way they run and in the integrity that they have. They are conceptual and they can see the reaction of consciousness in those they talk to, and the older ones right now can't. So we tell you that the dark and light balance is then going to change what? It eventually will change who you elect! And it's about time. Don't look for it immediately, but it's going to be there. Watch for more conceptual common sense campaigning, leaving behind the old style that you have had for 200 years.

Financial

This is a summary on this subject: You have attacked your own financial systems in the last five years to try and make them fair and to clean out as much of the greed as possible. Historians alive today will tell you that this would have been an impossible situation in the past, since big money was seen as untouchable. Yet you have disturbed the nest and started planting the seeds of a better system. This recession you're in is a recalibration of big money. You called them on it, and we told you it was coming almost a year before it happened. We even told you what would fall first [insurance] and that it would be one of the largest insurance companies on the planet [and it was].

So think about this for a moment. We could see it coming because energy is like that. It creates slow, strong potentials that can be predicted. It's not over, either, since the old system has to recreate itself. Perhaps you've noticed that your bankers are confused, if you've noticed. It doesn't matter what the government says they are allowed to do, or how much money they are being given to do it. They're not doing it! They are frozen in the headlights of a new paradigm and don't know how to operate. That should tell you how new and uncertain this change is – like nothing you have seen.

Now that, my dear Human Being, is a shift of dark and light. Do you see this? Integrity won out over abundance and power, and the system gets altered. It may get altered again, but there'll come a day when the ones who have the money to lend must create win-win situations, instead of greed-based systems. You haven't even seen these systems yet, but you will. You won't believe some of the ideas that the Indigos will think of for banking where everybody wins, and there won't be those left behind, scratching their heads and asking, *"What happened to my house?"* New systems are coming, and they won't be ones that are in your economic textbooks.

The Planet's Economy

There'll come a time on the planet when there'll probably be no more than five currencies. Unity is the way of all things; it is the structure that creates succinctness in integrity, power of trade, and ease of working. Entire continents will band together as a trading group, and there will be far fewer rules and details to wade through and, therefore, it will be efficient and involve fewer money changers. This also helps to eliminate the very poor, since they will now be more involved in what happens in their own lands. That is what the earth is awakening to. It may take two generations before this has been realized and seen accurately, but you'll wake up one day and realize what you've done. You are putting things together instead of tearing them apart. That's counterintuitive to the old Human process!

In the next two decades, somebody will awaken and say, *"Hey, we didn't have a world war. Isn't that something? And we're not going to, either, because everybody is trading with everybody. We may have found a balance that works!"* Perhaps someone will even rename the "doomsday clock" something else, since it seems to be running backwards.

It's the Pollyanna approach, isn't it? Many think so and feel it's foolish. There will always be those who would argue and say, *"Kryon, it's not accurate and it's naïve. It's only a matter of time before we wipe ourselves out and have Armageddon. After all, that's what Humans do."* Well, dear ones, that's what Humans used to do! It's up to you whether you listen to those representing "the way it was" or not. They'll say, *"The earth is coming to an end."* There will even be those who will hang on to the last possible moment to say that December 21st [the year of this channel, 2012] will be the end of the earth.

So I have something for you to do for them. On December 22, 2012, just call them and remind them that their drama is over and the earth is still here. Now perhaps they can join you in planting seeds for peace on Earth, instead of wallowing in that which creates tension, fear and anxiety. Some of them may just do it. Others will miss the drama and continue to look for something else to fear. There will always be conspiracists and doomsayers aplenty. They won't like the Kryon message.

Prediction

And now for a prediction: I would not give you the following information if it were not in the works. I cannot give you a time-frame for this prediction because Spirit has no clock. We don't know what time it is. Time is a three-dimensional construct of your own creation. It serves you for your survival, and it has to be there. In 3D, you can't get from A to B unless you have a clock. In a quantum state, there is no A to B. In a quantum state, you're always in both places, so clocks do not exist. God has no clock. That is why when you get information from Sprit about doing something in your life, you must wait for synchronicity instead of rushing out and trying to do it *now*. Spiritual revelations do not carry an implication to go *do it now*. Instead, these are messages of the revelation of potentials that you will experience on your own time through those you meet and the synchronicities you create.

You have something inappropriate in your country. It's big and it has to do with big money, and it's going to fall. Perhaps in an unusual way, it will fall. I cannot tell you when, but I will tell you it's ripe with potential failure. Years ago, I told you when everybody can talk to everybody, there can be no more conspiracies. You got to see this same attribute years ago in another industry you call tobacco, where they were very big business. But under the hood, as you might say, the integrity was not there, for they were addicting young people to the product they were selling and it was making an entire population unhealthy and even setting up early death.

The result was that your country stopped purchasing the product en masse, and today the industry survives by selling to those countries that are not yet aware of what you found out. What took place was *the power of integrity over money*. We bring you this to show you what may very well happen again, for this is the prediction. Big pharma [the drug companies of America] is going to have to change very soon or collapse. When you have an industry that keeps people sick for money, it cannot survive in the new consciousness.

The big money that is involved in this closed circle is immense, and the lack of integrity is going to be revealed, slowly. The lives "lost for profit" will be counted, and there are going to be embarrassed faces, and even a suicide or two. To think of an industry that's supposed to cure people, keeping them sick on purpose will be a wound in the very fabric of what is correct and for the good of humanity.

So they will fall and you'll know their names and they're going to have to scramble to keep up with the rest of the world who may not have the proclivities for greed that made these fall. This may also change the perception of which countries have the best health inventions and solutions, and many in this country may turn to overseas answers for their health needs.

That's the prediction. When it starts to happen, dear one, and perhaps the movie starts it [the one that's in the works that is a secret], I want you to remember where you heard it first. Perhaps this information, given in advance, will solidify that this is real – that the channelling you hear today comes from the source that we say it does, the one inside you.

When you're not here, you're with me. I know your face and I know who you really are. I know your real name, not the one you've got right now. That is the truth of the day. Recalibration is upon you in so many ways. We'll continue this information, this cycle of revelation, and many more things will be revealed. It's time. That's the energy of 2012.

And so it is.

Kryon

When you are in touch with your Higher-Self, you are in touch with all the parts of you. Sometimes Humans think that they're getting messages from angels, and these angels are given messages from other angels, and so on and so forth. Humans see a hierarchy of authority in everything, since it exists in their own reality. But with God, there's no such thing, for the wisdom of God is a singular wisdom, which is always the same and is fully present all the time, everywhere. The truth is the truth, and because you have a piece of God in you, you become aware of an absolute truth as you awaken spiritually. This is why you can take an awakened Human Being from another part of the world that is foreign to you, speaking another language that is not yours, and find the same truth. The God inside you is the same as the one inside them.

Kryon

From Chapter Fourteen
"The Three Winds"

Controversy!

Should I do this or that? How should I worship or be with the "correct" people? What about eating the "right" food, or using doctors and medicines? What is proper? Does God really care? Some of the answers here may surprise you. It's all part of a recalibration of attitude!

Lee Carroll

Chapter Six
THE RECALIBRATION OF "SHOULDS"
The Kryon Patagonia Cruise
January 2012

Kryon
Book 13

Chapter Six
The Recalibration of "Shoulds"
Live Kryon Channelling - January 2012

Greetings, dear ones, I am Kryon of Magnetic Service. Have you started to feel it yet? There's a difference in your perception, which makes it easier for you to come along with me to a quantum place. The ship [Cruise Ship] isolates you from the land just enough to suspend the reality of your everyday life. By the time you end this cruise, you will have bonded with the family with an energy of joy. Some solutions will be at hand, there will be a few epiphanies, and right now there is the potential for three healings. For some, peace will be delivered, replacing anxiety. There'll be some clarity on future plans as well, all because you sat together with me here today.

Your willingness to do this creates a state that is a different paradigm, a different way of being, an allowance for clearer thinking. The more often you do it, the more often you will feel the shift. So I want you to enjoy this moment and relax in it, knowing it is indeed safe and appropriate and proper. Dear ones, open your hearts this day, and let us do some exercises in spiritual logic.

This will not be a long channelling, but I'll do some information transfer for you. I will call this the recalibration of "shoulds" – things you feel you should do or should not do according to those who are in charge. *"In charge of what?"* you might ask. Well, they are the ones who are in charge of "shoulds", and you know who *they* are. They are tradition, spiritual authority, history and the learning of the past. The information I give is specific for *every should*, but not necessarily what you have been taught. Things are changing, and with the recalibration of energy on the planet, the puzzle you have worked on for a long time as a Lightworker is starting to shift as well. There are only a few questions about the *shoulds* to cover today, but they will be questions that are answered easily, but asked quite often. They cover a lot of different kinds of subjects.

Worship

Let's start with a spiritual one: God is the creator of the world, correct? Indeed, He is. Indeed, She is. Should not the creator then be worshipped? All of mankind has seen this fact and has, therefore, worshipped the idea of God in many forms from the very beginning. In the New Age esoteric movement, there is no worship. There truly are no grand altars or buildings. There is no place to kneel and give God thanks for anything. So some might face off with you and point their fingers and say, *"You are not worshipping as you should."* What is the answer to this? And what would you say?

I've given the metaphor before: Do you believe you are a piece of the Creator? The masters who walked the planet have told you that you are. One of the most recent ones, the Christ, identified himself and He said, *"I AM the Son of God,"* and then he looked up and said, *"And so are you."* So it is the great "I AM" that is inside you, but this is difficult to see or understand, for Humans look for grandness in divinity. They look for what they expect would be God in the sky, but they do not see that attribute inside themselves.

So let us redefine the "I AM". Let us decide what the *Son of God* terminology means. It means you are related to the Creator. It means that the Creator may very well be a family member. It means that you have information and understanding inside that you are, indeed, a family member. You have tranquility, lack of drama and safety when you think about what is inside yourself.

So that which is inside the Human is not necessarily felt as the grandness of the creator, but the *family* of the creator. So I ask, how do you treat your biological family? Which one have you worshipped lately? Mother? Father? Sister? Brother? And you would say, *"No, we do not worship one another. We respect one another. We look forward to being with certain family members. Sisters and brothers. There's no drama, but rather there is often the expectation of fun, enjoyment and joy. We care about one another. We love one another."* And that, dear one, is the answer to this *should!*

Instead of worship, there's appreciation, acknowledgment, ceremonies of thanks and love. That is a big difference from "down on your knees" worship, don't you see? Why not emulate the Master's words? If you are a Son or Daughter of God, then don't worship God. Instead, be part of the family. Appreciate that which is inside. Feel close to the Creator when you sit in the chair and do not elevate that which should not be elevated. Instead, love that which is inside yourself.

Communal Living for Strength

Here's another one: Some of you have been told that it makes more sense for Lightworkers to clump together, for logically, this would create more light. It would make more sense because Lightworkers would be of like mind and come together as a group and live together as a group. They could then better build that city as a group which has been called the *light on the hill*.

In addition, grouping together will create better communication, teaching and protection against the older energies of Earth and those things that would get in the way of the path of a true Lightworker. Is there anything wrong with this? Now I will tell you that those who would say this to you are in an old, linear paradigm. They're looking for things they feel will build a greater life, but have lost sight of what a Lightworker really does.

You are learning to be a self-sufficient creator of life. You could walk into the wilderness and contain all that is. This is the core of the statement, "I AM that I AM." The statement is not, "I am that I am, as long as they are what they are." You see? You are a self-sufficient lighthouse! When is the last time you saw a great deal of lighthouses all on one rock? They don't need each other! When is the last time you saw a lighthouse convention?

"Well, that's silly," you might say. *"Lighthouses are all anchored on rocks. They cannot come and visit one another."* Correct, but they can certainly send light to one another, could they not? After all, that's what a Lighthouse is equipped for. Perhaps Lightworkers can even be *entangled* with one another quantumly, and then distance would not matter? [quantum entanglement was mentioned in the seminar] So perhaps it's time for you to change the paradigm of how you imagine your place on the planet. Do you need protection? Is your light in danger?

When you leave this place and the boat that you are on docks for its final time on your cruise, you will all scatter. You'll go all over the world. Some of you will go unwillingly with tears in your eyes and you will say, *"I liked this. I would like to stay doing this."* But I can tell you that you are looking at an old paradigm to have sorrow at all! Once you have touched the heart of another, it's for life if you want it to be. You can connect and stay connected if you want. Your meeting here may create a network of light as you return to those places where you anchor yourself on your own rock and, all by yourself, create light in a dark place where you might live. Do you understand?

There is no *should* to live together as a group. If you were to do such a thing, it leaves the rest of the planet in the dark! It is incredibly self-serving and does nothing for anyone but the group. Those who do it just want to feel good with each other, and it does not help the planet. That's the second should.

Spiritual Eating – What Food Is For You?

Let us change the subject. *"Kryon, what should I eat as a Lightworker? I've heard many ideas. There are the ones who eat meat and the ones who do not, the ones who remove themselves from all things processed, and those who don't. There are even those who eat nothing at all and only breathe air! What is the thing I should do to honor God and my body with the food I eat?"*

Immediately there will be those who point to many spiritual scriptures and say, *"This is what you should do."* Others, less spiritual, may give you pure chemistry for cleansing and diet and health. Still others will stick with the tradition of your family heritage or ponder the integrity of eating an animal. So where is the truth in this? It appears to have logic and makes sense to many.

Dear ones, what is the goal? Is it to be healthy and, at the same time, honor God? Most would say, *"Yes."* All right, it's time for some spiritual logic. Question: Where did we establish that God was? Answer: The Creator is inside you. So how do you honor that divine plan that is inside you? The answer is to stay alive as long as you can! It's to hold your light on the planet as long as you can. So how can I give one dietary "should" to all of you who are so unique and different? For that matter, how could anyone give a generic instruction about one "correct diet" to such a vast array of different Human body types? Yet they do.

Here's the answer: Inside each of you there's something called *innate*. Innate is "body intelligence". Innate is the energy of body consciousness you use when you do "muscle testing" [kinesiology]. Innate knows what's happening at the very cellular level of your own body, which you do not know. Innate is the consciousness of your DNA itself. It's the ultimate source for your own "body awareness".

Innate knows about something called *Akashic inheritance.* This is the knowledge of *who* you used to be in past lives. All your dietary needs, to stay alive longer with health, are based on a cellular structure that *knows* what it wants and needs, and it "needs" what it is used to, dear ones.

It doesn't matter who you are or where you live. If you have arrived on this planet from a past lifetime in India, you're going to want to eat like an Indian – even if you are in Montana! If you had spent lifetimes in Asia, and today you're from Brooklyn, you might still want to eat like an Asian. Your chemistry "remembers" and craves what it feels will satisfy efficient digestion and health.

Your Akashic inheritance is far stronger than you give it credit for. Past life energies are NOT in the past! They are a quantum energy of your spiritual makeup that is *current* and something you carry around as part of your "whole self" this time around. They affect you!

The body will tell you that very thing, if you ask it. Your cellular structure will cry out for those things that you are used to, and will make your body relax and be comfortable with the chemistry it is used to. If you are new to this culture and spent the last five lifetimes in another one, don't be surprised if the former culture's diet is what you crave. The vegetarian diet will be something that serves you you're in touch with your Akash. You are eating what your cellular structure thrives on, not what someone told you to eat to make you more spiritual.

Pay attention to your body intelligence, for it will tell you a lot about who you've been. There is no *should* except one: Stay alive and be healthy. Listen to your cellular structure and it will tell you what you should eat. Is this not spiritual logic for you? Do not try to convert another to your "correct way" of eating. Honor the Akashic system and realize that your innate knows far better than you do what will work for you. My partner is currently attempting the "Glutton Free" diet. [Kryon humor]

Doctors and Drugs or Spiritual Methods?

"Dear Kryon, I have heard that you should stay natural and not use the science on the planet for healing. It does not honor God to go to a doctor. After all, don't you say that we can heal with our minds? So why should we ever go to a doctor if we can do it ourselves? Not only that, my doctor isn't enlightened, so he has no idea about my innate or my spiritual body needs. What should I do?"

First, Human Being, why do you wish to put so many things in boxes? You continue to want a yes and no answer for complex situations due to your 3D, linear outlook on almost everything. Learn to think out of the 3D box! Look at the heading of this section [above]. It asks which *one* should you do. It already assumes you can't do both because they seem dichotomous.

Let's use some spiritual logic: Here is a hypothetical answer, "Don't go to a doctor, for you can heal everything with your mind." So now I will ask: How many of you can do that in this room right now? How many readers can do that with efficiency right now? All of you are old souls, but are you really ready to do that? Do you know how? Do you have really good results with it? Can you rid yourself of disease and chemical imbalance with your mind right now?

I'm going to give you a truth, whether you choose to see it or not. You're not ready for that! You are not yet prepared to take on the task of full healing using your spiritual tools. Lemurians could do that, because Pleiadians taught them how! It's one of the promises of God, that there'll come a day when your DNA works that efficiently and you will be able to walk away from drug chemistry and the medical industry forever, for you'll have the creator's energy working at 100 percent, something you saw within the great masters who walked the earth.

This will be possible within the *ascended* earth that you are looking forward to, dear one. Have you seen the news lately? Look out the window. Is that where you are now? We are telling you that the energy is going in that direction, but you are not there yet.

Let those who feel that they can heal themselves begin the process of learning how. Many will be appreciative of the fact that you have some of the gifts for this now. Let the process begin, but don't think for a moment that you have arrived at a place where every health issue can be healed with your own power. You are students of a grand process that eventually will be yours if you wish to begin the quantum process of talking to your cells. Some will be good at this, and some will just be planting the seeds for it.

Now, I would like to tell you how Spirit works and the potentials of what's going to happen in the next few years. We're going to give the doctors of the planet new inventions and new science. These will be major discoveries about the Human body and of the quantum attributes therein.

Look at what has already happened, for some of this science has already been given to you and you are actually using it. Imagine a science that would allow the heart to be transplanted because the one you have is failing. Of course! It's an operation done many times a month on this planet. That information came from the Creator, did you realize that? It didn't drop off the shelf of some dark energy library to be used in evil ways.

So, if you need a new heart, Lightworker, should you go to the doctor or create one with your mind? Until you feel comfortable that you can replace your heart with a new one by yourself, then you might consider using the God-given information that is in the hands of the surgeon. It will save your life, and create a situation where you stay and continue to send your light to the earth! Do you see what we're saying?

You can also alter that which is medicine [drugs] and begin a process that is spectacular in its design, but not very 3D. I challenge you to begin to use what I would call the homeopathic principle with major drugs. If some of you are taking major drugs in order to alter your chemistry so that you can live better and longer, you might feel you have no choice. *"Well, this is keeping me alive,"* you might say. *"I don't yet have the ability to do this with my consciousness, so I take the drugs."*

In this new energy, there is something else that you can try if you are in this category. Do the following with safety, intelligence, common sense and logic. Here is the challenge: The principle of homeopathy is that an almost invisible tincture of a substance is ingested and is seen by your innate. Innate "sees" what you are trying to do and then adjusts the body's chemistry in response. Therefore, you might say that you are sending the body a "signal for balance." The actual tincture is not large enough to affect anything chemically – yet it works!

The body [innate] sees what you're trying to do and then cooperates. In a sense, you might say the body is healing itself because you were able to give it instructions through the homeopathic substance of what to do. So, why not do it with a major drug? Start reducing the dosage and start talking to your cells, and see what happens. If you're not successful, then stop the reduction. To your own amazement, you may often be successful over time.

You might be able to take the dosage that you're used to and cut it to at least a quarter of what it was. It is the homeopathic principle and it allows you to keep the purpose of the drug, but reduce it to a fraction of a common 3D dosage. You're still taking it internally, but now it's also *signaling* in addition to working chemically. The signal is sent, the body cooperates, and you reduce the chance of side effects.

You can't put things in boxes of yes or no when it comes to the grand system of Spirit. You can instead use spiritual logic and see the things that God has given you within the inventions and processes on the planet. Have an operation, save your life, and stand and say, *"Thank you, God, for this and for my being born where these things are possible."* It's a complicated subject, is it not? Each of you is so different from the other! You'll know what to do, dear one. Never stress over that decision, because your innate will tell you what is appropriate for you if you're willing to listen.

God doesn't change. Stay with tradition

Let us look at the final one. There are those who will tell you that God is the same yesterday, today and forever. They would say you should not, therefore, be in a New Age movement, for God will never change and the energy of God will always be the same. Therefore, your ideas of the energy shifting and God changing are foolishness. Then they will warn you and say, *"Stay away from the New Age and instead go with the traditions and the systems of religion and spiritual learning that are set up and have a history with billions of people on the earth."*

This entire argument above is based on a misunderstanding, dear ones. Here is the statement I wish to make. God is the same yesterday, today and forever. It's beautiful, for God the creator will never change. What *is* changing, however, is the Human Being's relationship to an unchanging God. What is changing is the Human Being's ability to get past an older energy and, with a new energy, meet the creator inside. It is the Human Being who is changing, not God.

The very environment around you is cooperating [Gaia] in order to better understand a God who is the same yesterday, today and forever. The New Age is about Human Beings recognizing that their relationship to Spirit is changing and becoming more real in their lives. This means that Humans can now begin to see and feel the creator inside in a new, profound way. New spiritual tools are at hand and an awareness of self is beginning to slowly increase. Humans are changing! God is the same.

Remove yourself from tradition, for it will only keep you in a prison of your own making, where you cling to mythology and never see the magnificence of your own soul.

The ONE Should

You might say there is one attribute that runs all through the *shoulds*. You *should* always allow yourself spiritual discernment in all things. Do not compartmentalize the energies around you, – something your linear mind wishes to do. Instead, meld these things into a soup of spiritual logic that makes sense for your life. Do not apply your rules to any other Human Being, but instead find out what works for you and celebrate it as you become more healthy.

Dear ones, I am the brother/sister Kryon. I know you. It doesn't matter whether you are young or an elder in this group. All of you are old souls who will be together a very long time. Remember this. The first month of 2012. The beginning of many new things.

And so it is.

Predictions!

Everyone loves them. Look on page 127. We are going to lose a Pope soon? Hey, we already did! Indeed, only 12 months after this channelling, the current Pope resigned, and Francis took over. Perhaps some of the other predictions will now be a little more interesting because of this? (smile).

Lee Carroll

Chapter Seven
THE RECALIBRATION OF FREE CHOICE
Dallas, Texas
Feruary 2012

Kryon
Book 13

Chapter Seven
The Recalibration of Free Choice
Live Kryon Channelling - February 2012

Greetings, dear ones, I am Kryon of Magnetic Service. The meetings with Humans who show up in anticipation of my visit are mostly made up of old souls. This was foreseen. Over two decades ago, when my partner began, the meetings contained curious souls. So it has evolved. It is the seriousness of the old soul that brings them to a room like this or to a place like this where they can listen or read. Spirit responds to potentials on my side of the veil, and again I say that we have no clock. We see the reader in the same way we see the one in the chair today. We see potentials as reality. That reality we now see brought you reading this on paper or on an electronic device. All this seems to us as within the same time frame that a few of you are experiencing in this meeting as you listen. So your future is our now.

We do not see empirical rules in our reality, but instead we see potentialities of existence. That is to say that we know who you are – listening, reading, or here in the chair. You think you know how many are here, but you don't know really what *here* means, for there are far more than you think. Does your *here* include the future? Does your here include generations to come? You see, anyone who ever listens to or reads these words, no matter when, is a potential that exists in our now. So that is what we discuss today, and we're going to call this *The Recalibration of Free Choice.*

We pause for a moment. There's a dispensation at this moment, no matter what the teaching is, no matter what the words are. Listen, reader: I know who you are. There's a dispensation right here for you. Before you get up out of the chair where you are, you can be different. It's because you will receive an energy that is being broadcast by us no matter what time you think it is or where you are – into the very quantum information of your DNA, the patterning of your soul. The very Akash of your Higher-Self and your soul energy are involved. It's an awakening that will last for the rest of your lifetimes, because you make a decision today. This is how profound free choice is for a Human.

The Human can *turn on a dime*. Oh, look at your history! Look what you've done in these last years. Governments that are inappropriate have fallen (or are falling); financial systems that are inappropriate have fallen. However, you continue to ask, *"Where is the change?"* It's all around you, dear one, but it's slow and didn't happen in the last weeks. So be patient and allow the wheels of shift to turn at their own pace.

Free Choice Isn't That Simple

Free choice would seem to be a simple aspect. Free choice to a Human Being means that you have free will to choose anything you want. But it isn't that way at all. You can only choose things you can conceive of or that you *think* you can change. You cannot choose things that do not appear to you to be choosable. For instance, rats in a maze have free choice. They can go anywhere they want to. But one of the choices that never occurs to a rat is to remove the matrix. It's not in their consciousness or their reality because they have solid walls before them that represent the maze. So they simply try to choose a direction within the walls and the puzzle in front of them.

Humans live in a perception of a dimensionality, much like an example of living in black and white instead of color. You might say Humans have always had free choice in black and white, yet they're not aware of color. So if you don't have color, you are not going to choose red or blue or green. Understand? Now, imagine for a moment that those colors are a multi-dimensional reality. Therefore, the Human Being (although s/he has free choice) can't even conceive of the things that s/he cannot conceive of. So s/he doesn't choose a color, because s/he doesn't know it exists. So that, dear ones, is what is changing. You're going to start to see concepts that never were concepts! Prepare for color!

I'm going to give you a little list of what to expect, and some of you will see these things quickly and some not for a while. I will give you an overview with no clock. So when you say, *"Well, dear Kryon, when are these things going to happen?"* I'll say, "Yes." Oh, dear one, they're going to happen, for we see the potentials of all of them happening, which means we see your manifestation already there.

Spirituality

Number one: Spirituality. The systems of spiritual design on your planet are starting to change. This is not telling you that certain ones are going to go away. They're simply going to change. Some of the largest spiritual systems on the planet, which you would call organized religion, are shifting. They're going to shift away from that which is authority on the outside to authority on the inside. It will eventually be a different way of worship, slowly changing the rules while keeping the basic doctrine the same.

The doctrine of the Christ has always been to find the God inside. The teachings were clear. The examples of the miracles were given as an example of what humans could do, not to set a man up for worship as a God. So when that has been absorbed, the teachings of Jesus can remain the teaching of the Jesus. It simply changes the interpretation.

The teachings of the great prophets of the Middle East (all related to each other) are about unity and love. So once the holy words are redefined with new wisdom, the Human changes, not the words of the prophets. In fact, the prophets become even more divinely inspired and their wisdom becomes even more profound.

You're going to lose a pope soon. I have no clock. Soon to us can mean anything to you. The one who replaces him may surprise you, for his particular organization will be in survival mode at that point in time. That is to say that fewer and fewer are interested in starting the priesthood. Fewer and fewer young people are interested in the organization, and the new pope must make changes to keep his church alive. That means that his organization will remain, but with a more modern look at what truly is before all of you in a new energy. It is not the fall of the church. It is instead the recalibration of the divinity inside that would match the worship that goes on. It's a win-win situation. The new pope will have a difficult time, since the old guard will still be there. There could even be an assassination attempt, for the way of the old energy dies hard. That is number one. Watch for it. It's a change in the way spiritual systems work. It's a realignment of spiritual systems that resound to a stronger truth that is Human-driven, rather than prophet-driven.

Drama

Number two: Against everything you think is Human nature, Human Beings are going to start to react differently to drama. At the moment, drama is attractive. You're seeing your media on its last gasp of reality, giving you reality programs so you can watch drama, as though you didn't have enough of it at home. I want you to watch for this shift, because it's going to tell you that there is a shift taking place in basic Human nature. Eventually, these current things are not going to be attractive at all. Not at all. There'll come a time when you look backwards in time and you will see when you watched those particular kinds of entertainment and say, *"How barbaric that was!"* It's going to change.

This means that a shift in what Human Beings want to see as their entertainment is at hand. It's a shift in what they want to experience in their lives and in their free time. There will be more of a motivation to watch the things that soothe their souls, instead of the drama that mixes them up. They will not be fed anymore by what used to feed them in the old energy. If you turn on a television show that was produced in the '50s, how do you like it? Does it seem trite and laughable in its innocence? It does, and that's due to a shift of your reality today. So an actual shift of how Human Beings react to drama will be coming.

You're not going to be as interested in things that are dramatic, but rather you're going to be more interested in things that are informative and heartwarming. That's coming. I know, some of you will say, *"I doubt it, because Humans are Humans."* Some will even argue and they'll say, *"Well, Kryon, most of humanity, you have said, are not old souls. So, therefore, they won't shift along with us. So how can most of humanity shift?"* I'll tell you this: There are some things that will be worldwide and there are going to be some things that are only *old-soul wide.* You'll see. But the seeds are planted first with you. So what you feel and what you do will eventually be seen in the general population. How do you feel right now about what is on television, old soul? You're already objecting! You're already seeing the barbarism. You're already seeing those who have no integrity in their journalism and wish to scare you instead of inform you. That is going to shift. You will demand it.

Think of it this way: The old souls are the seeds who plant an energy that grows and allows new seeds to be made. Eventually, even the young souls will have an allowance for this *seed inheritance,* which the new energy of the earth is providing. That was number two.

Longer Life is Going to Happen, But...

Number Three: Here is one that is a review. We keep bringing it up because Humans don't believe it. If you're going to start living longer, there are those who are frightened that there will be overpopulation. You've seen the way it is so far, and the geometric progression of mathematics is absolute and you cannot change it. So if you look at the population of the earth and how much it has shifted in the last two decades, it's frightening to you. What would change that progression?

The answer is simple, but requires a change in thinking. The answer is *a civilization on the planet who understands a new survival scenario.* Instead of a basic population who has been told to have a lot of children to enhance the race [old survival], they begin to understand the logic of a new scenario. The Akashic wisdom of the ages will start to creep in with a basic survival scenario shift. Not every single woman will look at herself and say, *"The clock is ticking,"* but instead can say, *"I have been a mother 14 times in a row. I'm going to sit this one out."* It's a woman who understands that there is no loss or guilt in this, and actually feels that the new survival attribute is to keep the family small or not at all! Also, as we have said before, even those who are currently ignorant of population control will figure out what is causing babies to be born [Kryon joke].

Part of the *New Africa* will be education and healing, and eventually a zero population growth, just like some of the first-world nations currently have. Those who are currently tied to a spiritual doctrine will actually see that doctrine changed regarding Human birth – watch for it. Then they will be able to make a free choice that is appropriate even within the establishment of organized religion. You see, things are going to change where common sense will say, *"Perhaps it would help the planet if I didn't have children or perhaps just one child."* Then the obvious, *"Perhaps I can exist economically better and be wiser with just one. It will help the one!"* Watch for these changes. For those of you who are steeped in the tradition of the doctrines and would say that sounds outrageously impossible, I give you the new coming pope [Kryon smile]. For those of you who feel that uncontrolled procreation is inevitable, I encourage you to see statistics you haven't seen or didn't care to look at yet about what first-world countries have already accomplished on their own, without any mandates. It's already happening. That was number three.

Energy (again)

Number four: The natural resources of the planet are finite and will not support the continuation of what you've been doing. We've been saying this for a decade. Watch for increased science and increased funding for alternate ways of creating electricity (finally). Watch for the very companies who have the most to lose being the ones who fund it. It is the beginning of a full realization that a change of thinking is at hand. You can take things from Gaia that are energy, instead of physical resources. We speak yet again about geothermal, about tidal, about wind. Again, we plead with you not to over-engineer this. For one of the things that Human Beings do in a technological age is to over-engineer simple things. Look at nuclear – the most over-engineered and expensive steam engine in existence!

Your current ideas of capturing energy from tidal and wave motion don't have to be technical marvels. Think paddle wheel on a pier with waves, which will create energy in both directions [waves coming and going] tied to a generator that can power dozens of neighborhoods, not full cities. Think simple and decentralize the idea of utilities. The same goes for wind and geothermal. Think of utilities for groups of homes in a cluster. You won't have a grid failure if there is no grid. This is the way of the future, and you'll be more inclined to have it sooner than later if you do this, and it won't cost as much.

Water

We've told you that one of the greatest natural resources of the planet, which is going to shift and change and be mysterious to you, is fresh water. It's going to be the next *gold*, dear ones. So, we have also given you some hints and examples and again we plead: Even before the potentials of running out of it, learn how to desalinate water in real time without heat. It's there, it's doable, and some already have it in the lab. This will create inexpensive fresh water for the planet.

There is a change of attitude that is starting to occur. Slowly you're starting to see it, and the only thing getting in the way of it are those companies with the big money who currently have the old system. That's starting to change as well. The big money always wants to invest in what it knows is coming next, but it wants to create what is coming next within the framework of what it has "*on the shelf.*" What is on the shelf is oil, coal, dams, and non-renewable resource usage. It hasn't changed much in the last 100 years, has it? Now you will see a change of free choice. You're going to see decisions made in the boardrooms that would have curled the toes of those two generations ago. Now "the worst thing they could do" might become "the best thing they could do." That, dear ones, is a change of the free choice concept. When the thinkers of tomorrow see options that were never options before, that is a shift. That was number four.

Integrity That May Surprise...

Number five: There will be those who think it impossible to have a search for integrity and fairness in all things. In other words, Human Beings will not simply go with what they are told is the status quo. They will look at it and they will say, *"Well, I think it could be better. I'm going to look around for something that has more integrity and fairness."* Yes, there will be those who tell you, *"Look, the institutions hold all the cards and you have to do it their way. If you want health insurance or you want loans from the banks for your home, you better do it their way."* I have news for you. Even this is going to change.

"What are you going to do?" the Human asks. *"They hold all the power!"* In the past, there was nothing you could do. Now I'll tell you what the potentials are. You're going to pull out the puzzle and look past the walls of the maze. You're going to say, *"Well, then I'll start my own institution."* And some will. The new institutions, based on integrity, will sweep right past the old energy. In other words, those who are young today will be the ones who are going to start a new way of banking, a new way of health care, and a new way of insurance. And when you see these plans, you'll say, *"Why didn't we think of that?"*

Have you seen innovation and invention in the past decade that required thinking out of the box of an old reality? Indeed, you have. I can't tell you what's coming, because you haven't thought of it yet! But the potentials of it are looming large. Let me give you an example. Let us say that 20 years ago you predicted that there would be something called the Internet on a device you don't really have yet using technology that you can't imagine. You will have full libraries, buildings filled with books, in your hand – a worldwide encyclopedia of everything knowable, with the ability to look it up instantly! Not only that, but that lookup service isn't going to cost a penny! You can call friends and see them on a video screen, and it won't cost a penny! No matter how long you use this service and to what depth you use it, the service itself will be free.

Now, anyone listening to you back then would perhaps have said, *"Even if we can believe the technological part, which we think is impossible, everything costs something. There has to be a charge for it! Otherwise, how would they stay in business?"* The answer is this: With new invention comes new paradigms of business. You don't know what you don't know, so don't decide in advance what you think is coming based on an old energy world.

The Unthinkable... Politics, A Review

Humans will begin to search for integrity and fairness and it's going to happen in the places you never expect. I said this last week, so this is a review. There'll come a time when you will demand this of your politics – fairness and integrity. So when the candidates start calling each other names, you will turn your back on them and they won't get any votes. They're going to get the point real fast, don't you think? How about that?

Let me give you another potential. This country that I sit in right now [USA] will set the mold for that particular attribute. I have no clock. Watch for the youngsters to set this in motion, and they will, for they are the voters of tomorrow and they do not want the energy of today. To some of them, it's so abominable they won't even register to vote in this energy. You're going to see this soon. That was number five.

The News

Number six. I'll be brief. Watch for your news to change. It has to. When the media realizes that Human Beings are changing their watching habits, they're going to start changing what they produce for you to watch. Eventually, there's going to be something called "The Good News Channel," and it will be very attractive indeed. For it will be real and offset the drama of what is today's attraction. This is what families at night, sitting around the table, will wish to watch. They'll have something where the whole picture of a situation is shown and not just the dramatic parts. You will hear about what's happening on the planet that no one is telling you now, and when that occurs [we have no clock, dear one], it's going to compete strongly with the drama. I keep telling you this. Human nature itself is starting to be in color instead of black and white. Watch for it. And that was number six.

Predictions

There are two more. Very recently we gave you a prophecy of prediction. We reiterate it now. Right now on the planet there's something in the works that is going to bring *big pharma* to its knees. Much like what happened to the tobacco industry, where there was a realization of a lack of integrity, there was alarm and outrage. You saw an industry that knowingly addicted the young and caused death, and this was revealed. And it didn't take that long, did it? And we said this not too long ago, and I repeat: When you see an entire industry that, for monetary reasons, is willing to keep people sick for profit, it's going to fall over. Sooner than later. You're going to see the rumblings of it very soon.

You're going to start to see Human Beings look at their health in a different way. Do you know what the real answer to long-term health care is? Not only in this country, but the earth? I will give you a hint. Don't get sick! And that, dear Human Being, is what I'm going to tell you is at hand. Coming is an understanding of the body in a way you have not understood it before. Your DNA is built to regenerate and last for hundreds of years. Right now, you're here for a moment and you die. The research is there. The beginning of extended life is there. Human Beings are going to search for things that are natural and processes that have always existed, and that will have an avenue of opening because of the demise of big pharma. And you'll wonder why you didn't know it before and you will look back and cringe, like you do today with the ads of the '50s with the doctor smiling, recommending a certain kind of tobacco.

I don't have a clock, dear one. I cannot tell you when. I can only guarantee you it is going to happen. It has to. You cannot have systems that are that large that have no integrity existing in the new energy. Do you understand? Then there are those who will say, *"I hope it happens while I'm here."* Oh, it will. Maybe you won't be who you are today, but you'll be here to see it, old soul. [Kryon smile] And that was number seven.

The End of War

Number Eight: The last one is the best. For thousands of years on this planet, Human Beings have warred with each other. If you take a look at the reasons they warred with each other, you will quickly see there aren't any good ones – land, resources, greed, power. Those are not reasons. That is a description of old energy. Those are not reasons. Reasons would be perhaps defense against an aggressor. But what if there is no longer the consciousness of the aggressor?

When I appeared in my partner's life more than 20 years ago, I said to him privately that the first messages we're going to give will be unbelievable. There would be laughter. We told him that Human nature and consciousness itself would change, and that the seeds of peace would be planted and there would come a time where there is no more war. Indeed, the laughter was great because humans look at history and they see patterns based on an absolute energy called Human Nature. *"Impossible! There always has to be war. There always has been. Therefore, there always will be."* This is you, in a box, in a black and white potential, where you can only see the black and white of what is and the black and white of what has been. You have no idea the shades of color that are there in your consciousness and the beauty of the love of God.

North Korea is on the edge of change, as we told you it might be. What did this require? The death of the old energy, and I want you to watch this take place. The advisors of the young leader are going to do their best to pull him back into an old energy. This free choice of his will be far different from his father's, for he sees some color. Watch for these things. They'll take longer than you want, but it is the beginning of the beginning.

You'll see a fresh unification of South America sooner than not, for what is going to take place potentially this year in Venezuela. You'll see Iran changing. We have no clock. These are the potentials. These can change with free choice. These are not prophecies. This is a reality shift, dear ones, so number eight becomes the propensity not to war again. This is what Humans are going to want. This is what governments are going to want. There is a wisdom factor that will begin to manifest on the planet that is grander than what you think is possible. For when you look at government, what do you think about? Today you see dysfunction, and there is an axiom that says the more people who try to do something together, the worse it gets. It all settles to the lowest common denominator. I'm telling you even those things are going to become old energy concepts. Instead, you're going to watch wisdom become the top potential. And that is number eight.

I have no clock. I cannot tell you when. I can just tell you it is in the works, and there will be the seeds of it for you to observe soon – right now, in every single one of the eight categories I showed you.

There are those who will say, *"Well, Kryon, you're doing a lot more predictions than you used to."* I want to tell you what's going on, dear one. I am not predicting anything. I am just telling you what's already there in the potential soup of your reality. That's what Humans are doing on this planet, and for those who believe this communication, you should breathe a sigh of relief and say, *"It's about time."*

I'm about to leave yet again, but not before this admonition. Seed planters, you have 18 years to plant these new seeds. They will grow faster if you do it now rather than later. Your part to play is to have a higher consciousness in these areas at home and at work, and to show those around you what you know through your wisdom. Show them the love of God in your life by treating them as you would yourself – to be slow to anger and quick to forgive. Create solace around you, a bubble of peace around you that is so desirable that people will want to be with you. Be non-judgmental.

These are the seeds that will change the Crystalline Grid of this planet, and your children and their children are the ones who will inherit what you do today. This shift is about consciousness change; it's why you're here.

This is the truth of this day, and again, I say it: All things may pull backwards a bit before they move forward, but this is the way of things and always has been. If you look at the last 50 years, you will see a tremendous change in Human nature. However, it's nothing compared to what you're going to see.

I am Kryon. Twenty-two years ago, my partner let me into his life. I knew it would take four years for him to get going, and it did. Eighteen years ago was when the alignment started, and that's when the work began. I am here because of what humanity did. Kryon has always been on the planet, but only in the last 18 years were the messages profound about the shift. The grid alignment group arrived in 1989 and left in 2002 and the magnetics were set. Then Human consciousness began to shift as we said it would.

This is our message for today. Leave differently than you came.

And so it is.

Did your parents or grandparents expect to see the geopolitical system of the Cold War change so dramatically and quickly in the 1980s? It was against all odds and logic, and against all the prophecy of the planet. Why do you doubt that such changes could occur again? Have you seen the forgiveness and softening toward your previous enemies of World War II? If that can happen in as little as two generations, why do you doubt that religions might be able to do the same?

Do you really think you're going to have a planet where all of those thousands of years of spiritual teaching will simply vanish? It's not practical, is it? No, instead expect them to morph into something that is more cooperative and which is beautiful. Expect the differences to be understood and celebrated instead of warring over them. It's about time this happened, and it signals spiritual evolution and the evolution of consciousness on planet Earth.

This is the new Human Being and this is the future. You're starting to turn the corner through 2013 and beyond, and I've just given you a snapshot of what can be and what we say can take place.

Kryon

The Connection to Gaia

This subject demands a Kryon book by itself! Wait a minute, it actually has one! (see page 255). If we are recalibrating, and the Gaia energy is directly responsive to us, then Gaia is also recalibrating. Indeed, this is true, and most of the Ancients have prophesied this very thing. So what are the mechanics of it? How does it work? Read on...

Lee Carroll

Chapter Eight
THE RECALIBRATION OF GAIA
Melbourne, Australia
March 2012

Kryon

Book 13

Chapter Eight
The Recalibration of Gaia
Live Kryon Channelling - March 2012

Greetings, dear ones, I am Kryon of Magnetic Service. The family before me is known and I will say it yet again, that there is no mystery about who sits here and who may be listening or eventually who may be reading. It comes together in a timeless state, which is not the reality that you share at this moment. It's a reality that I have of a timeless place in a quantum state filled with the potentials of those I know who will hear and read this message. So, although it may seem for you in the room to be now, it is all now for me.

I wish I could take you back several thousand years. Slowly, as the time goes backwards, the buildings would disappear and everything would be reduced to dirt, and the indigenous would show themselves. If you took a look at what the indigenous were doing then, they had two things that they emphasized and two things that occupied all that was important to them. The first was the honoring of their ancestors, and the second was the honoring of Gaia.

The energies of the indigenous were focused on the land, but not just a land that would give them water or food, but the actual energy of the dirt of the earth. Many of you know of what I speak if you have studied their lives. It is no different from the indigenous all over Earth, for it was intuitive that Gaia is the energy of what you would call Mother Earth, and it was aligned with humanity in a society that was not nearly as complex as yours is now. Instead, they experienced the overwhelming energies of being in alliance with the planet and with those ancestors who had gone before.

I tell you this because the object of the lesson this day is how that alliance is still alive and changing. You may not see as they did, but the alliance is still there and it's there in ways that are mysterious to you. I'm going to help clear this up, and describe the system and how it all works. So do not be shocked or surprised if I start at the molecular level of the Human Being. I have to, for therein lie the mysteries.

The Connection between Gaia and the Human

Here is the premise, dear ones: "As goes consciousness, goes Gaia. As goes Gaia, goes DNA." There is a partnership involved here that is more than you think. The indigenous did not pray for rain. They did not pray for good crops and did not worship any deity. In their reality, they *felt* the planet and they knew that it was part of them. It was all there was. So they were always one with the planet, and the appearance of rain and crops were an alliance with Gaia, and they used ceremonies of alignment, not prayers of asking. If they didn't get what they wanted, they knew they were out of alignment. You are missing that attribute today, but the process of this alignment is still alive and it still works.

Let us speak of DNA yet again. The DNA molecule sits there and is unique. It is unique to all things, for there is a complement of divinity in it that the animals do not have. There are certain animals that have so many things – there are even animals designed to reincarnate, specific ones that do so for you as Humans. Yet they do not have souls as you, and they do not have the divine spark that you do. Their cycle is a cycle of love to support you.

The Reincarnation of Pets – A Gaia System

I speak now of something that I rarely speak of and you should know this: All of the systems of the planet revolve around you. This is a support system for Human Beings to make their lives easier and better as Gaia responds to what they give it. If you love an animal, you probably are aware that the animal's life is short – too short. Let me give you some information, and if you believe that this channelling is real, then believe this: Those animals that you fall in love with will come back to you. The very soul continues the love affair and, if you want to, it is there for you to find again – and that is a compassionate support system that honors that divinity inside a Human. Did you know that in your DNA is a quantum attribute that we have discussed for many years? My partner spoke of it just yesterday.

DNA Has a Quantum Field

Science is starting to see that it is it possible that the DNA molecule has attributes that actually give information to the spin of quantum structure in the Universe. So this means that DNA is a quantum engine. But now I wish to expand that picture for you, for DNA does not sit alone. It is a family, and in the Human body that family is more than 100 trillion strong in one Human Being. But you have the puzzle before you that science has never even looked at: How does DNA all "know" together? At the moment, science does not even see the need to study communication among DNA molecules. They haven't seen the field yet; they haven't seen the structure yet; and they haven't seen the shadows yet. [From Lee: The "shadows of the atom" were discovered one month after this channelling.]

DNA must work together in the Human body for the intelligence of what we call the *innate* of the Human body to function. All of DNA must work as one. From the top of your head to your toes, these molecules must act as one set of instructions. This is unique information, for there is no other Human Being on the planet who has your DNA. Therefore, you must acknowledge that there is something that must happen within your body that connects all the DNA together. Otherwise, you could not function.

There must be communication among DNA molecules. This is where the genes are produced, and this is where the information is that is your Higher-Self. This is the Akashic Record and it must all vibrate together as one, trillions of parts vibrating as one. So we say it to you, for physicists to see, and for them to understand finally that the Human Being has DNA that is in an *entangled state**. That is to say it is locked into one state and the parts behave as one.

The Entangled DNA of the Human Body

There is an attribute of physics that has not been seen or discussed yet and I give it here for the first time so you will understand a little bit more about how it works. But more than that, when it is discovered you will remember where you heard it. If you have multiple quantum fields around molecules, that means that they must overlap. So the fields overlap one another and you already have the science that shows you what happens – multiple overlapping magnetic fields occur. Magnetics represent quantum energies, so the results of the DNA are similar. There's *magic* that takes place, which even science does not understand, called inductance. In your everyday life, you see this when you look at the magnetic field of the sun, which is called the heliosphere (solar wind), interfering with the magnetic field of the earth, which is the magnetic grid. You get sparks! The Aurora Borealis. That is what happens when magnetic fields overlap. In this state, information is transmitted, and in electronics this attribute is well known and used every day.

Now, if you have not a magnetic field, but a quantum field around every molecule, I will tell you that you don't get sparks, you get a *designer entangled state*. Overlapping quantum fields are attributes that have not yet been studied, recognized, or measured.

---

* Entanglement is an attribute of quantum physics that is just now being explored at a macro level. Some kinds of entanglement create "quantum locking" and some do not. In the case of DNA, the information is "locked" amoung DNA molecules through the quantum attributes of the field.

When they do, they will see the mechanics of an entangled state that then creates an overall field around the Human Being that is much larger then you might expect. What might be in that field which is measured at 8 meters wide? And, has it ever been seen? The answer is yes! You'll find it in your scriptures, the old ones in Second Kings [Holy Bible]. For again we say it was Elisha who saw the master Elijah ascend of his own will, and on the ground his field glowed. It illuminated and he left the planet in a bubble of light, a vehicle, a "chariot of ascension," which took him. Elisha named the vehicle *Merkabah*, which means "to ride." So now you have a name for it, and one that is recognized not only by the Ancients in spiritual lands, but also to this day by those who see it with second sight. It is the quantum field of the Human Being – the Merkabah.

So the Merkabah is really a quantum field, and this field is filled with information. The information that it is filled with seems to be non-structured to you, but it actually is quite structured as we see it. It is the matrix of the templates of the Human Being him/herself, and it is ready and waiting to be altered by another quantum field, and that field is called consciousness. Now I haven't mentioned Gaia yet, have I? All of this is leading up to tell you something that I have only hinted at before on how it works.

So there sits the Human Being with all of this intact, which you can't see, that we just tell you about. Intangible, unmeasurable things are laughed at by science. Energy fields around humans? Next time a scientist starts to walk away from you, ask him for his compassion meter or his anxiety meter or his love meter. What? He doesn't have one? Does that mean none of those chemistry-altering emotions exist? No. Not only do they exist, but yes, they also can be measured, but not yet. Perhaps in the near future, the "what can't be measured, can't exist" paradigm will change.

The Human Quantum Field and the Innate System

Around every single Human Being is a beautiful field that some have even called magic, for in this field is not only your Akashic Record, but also the attributes of your Higher-Self (soul). It echoes what's inside the DNA molecule itself, and if you had quantum eyes you could look at a Human and read who they were, and who they used to be, and what their issues are. You would see what we call the *innate* of the Human Being, the very intelligence of cellular structure. There are those in the room who have that sight, and they are what you would call medical intuitives, past life readers, and more. Healers in this room depend upon this second sight, and they see it around the Human Being. It is no mystery. It's not magic; it's science. I still haven't mentioned Gaia yet, have I? I'm getting there.

The innate of the Human Being is the bridge between the intelligence of your cellular structure (and your DNA) and your 3D Human consciousness. There are those in the room that practice something called *kinesiology*. Now, kinesiology is a way to talk to innate. The Human Being is smart, but oddly enough, still not smart enough to know what is going on in his own body. We have said it before, and it's a mystery, isn't it? You can have a disease growing in your body right now, yet you're just smiling and having no idea about it until it hurts. Isn't that odd? But innate knows it at the outset.

You might have to use muscle testing (kinesiology) in order to find out what you're allergic to or what's going on in your system – a yes or no process. Isn't it interesting that you have to go through that process to discover what is happening in your own body? So you might say to yourself, *"Maybe something is missing? We should be able to know immediately what is happening in our own cellular structure!"* You'd be right. Indeed, there should be a bridge between all that information, which is quantum, and your consciousness. You'd be right. I haven't mentioned Gaia yet, have I? And here's where it gets good.

Gaia Energy is Driven by Humanity

Gaia cooperates with humanity. Gaia is always measuring the attributes of group humanity. When there were only a few Human Beings on the planet and when they were in touch with Gaia, Gaia responded. So did your DNA. It took its cue from Gaia in how well it worked. DNA, which is the blueprint of a Human, is designed to work with Gaia, and Gaia is designed to be reactive to Human consciousness. They are a closed system, and one always affects the other.

DNA is designed to give the Human Being a very long life and is also designed for full rejuvenation and self-healing. DNA is designed so that the bridge between you and the innate is *always there*. Yet that's not the way it is, is it? You've heard of those Human Beings of old who lived a great many years. Was that a misprint in scripture? No. So what allowed some Human Beings to actually have more healthy years back then than now? Was that true about their ages? I will tell you: Yes, it was, and here's why. The field around you and others is so aligned with Gaia that you cooperate and shift according to one another. It's what the Ancients knew, and it is why they were *one with the planet*. This is something that you are going to start discovering as well.

Gaia takes its cue from Human consciousness for the *energy to create* on the planet. We have told you that for 22 years. It also goes the other way, for your DNA as a whole responds to something called the *Crystalline Grid* of the planet. It's an esoteric "memory grid" which contains the stored energy and events of humanity. We've given you teachings about the Crystalline Grid before, but you might say it is a shell around the dirt of the earth that is not seen but that holds all of the energies and history of anyone who has ever lived on the planet. When you are born, and at your first breath, the quantum field of your humanness looks at the Crystalline Grid and adjusts its efficiency for the energy of the planet. humanity has been created in this energy in the time it has been here.

Right now, the energy on this planet is filled with millenniums of war, old energy fighting, machismo, and intolerance. This, then, is what the DNA adjusts to at your birth. Whereas you are designed for 100 percent DNA efficiency, right now it's at 30 percent. And that, dear one, is what is changing, for the DNA is now starting to operate at a higher efficiency because there's a consciousness shift going on. You're seeing it first, of course, with the ones who are currently being born. At their first breath, they're now at 35 percent, and this translates into a Human Being that is far more aware and more conceptual at a far earlier age. It's almost as though they have an instinctual awareness of overall Humanism, instead of having to learn it all over again, as you did.

We have told you about these new children, and that is why your children are so unusual – and you know they are. Many in the audience who have grandchildren are really seeing it; the kids are different. So you might say, *"Well, it's too bad that we can't raise our DNA efficiency ourselves."* Well, you can! For the energy of the planet is alert and ready to send the signal to the old soul who starts to understand that they can change their own fields through the templates that float in them, through consciousness, pure intent, and through compassion. You can change the quantum "print" of DNA with compassion! We have said that from the beginning, so let me summarize this in simple words that are not scientific. Go slow, my partner. Make this succinct. [Kryon talking to Lee]

New DNA Adjustment to New Gaia Energy

When you're born, your DNA adjusts itself to what has happened on the earth. It has created a reality for you that you call *Human Nature*. The earth changes, and now the Crystalline Grid is actually lifting the veil slightly, and your DNA is starting to respond. The first response will be seen within your children, and they are already coming in with a different conceptual Human attribute. They don't think in the same linear fashion you do. Have you noticed?

This is going to change more and more as time goes by. Eventually, there will be a much more efficient DNA that creates the missing bridge between the innate and the normal Human brain. That means that you will have more intuitive thoughts about what is wrong and right within your own cellular structure. Some of you will discover different eating habits for the first time, and you'll be tuned in to a cellular structure that says, *"If I change this and that, I'm going to live longer."* The result will be instinctive eating changes that have no explanation. Your innate is starting to communicate.

Habits that you've had for years will start to drop away because your cellular structure will start to help you eliminate them, knowing they don't suit you. Don't be surprised if one of them is overeating and metabolic adjustments to bring your body weight into line without the discomfort of extreme diets. Others are the dropping of substances that you are addicted to, and within that process is an allowance that lets you live much longer.

You will see a regeneration of cellular structure that will surprise you. You'll heal faster and you'll know it. You'll start to see a situation where you're less sick than you've ever been in your life. The prevailing 3D wisdom will tell you, *"Well, you're older now, so you're going to get sick more."* But you won't, and you'll know that something is changing. So what we're saying to you, dear ones, is that you can have the same things that the youngsters have. You will now slowly awaken to a new energy on this planet, which will allow you to live longer. Your DNA is going to start cooperating in a more efficient way. 35 percent? Perhaps even 40 percent, old soul? It's on its way to something far higher.

The prophet Elijah, Jesus, the master Christ, Buddha, Mohammad, Paramahansa Yogananda, and many more had DNA working at 90 to 100 percent. All of them chose the way they wished to use it, and you could see it in them and feel it in them. The prophet Elijah chose to leave the planet through an ascended status of his own design and choosing. That's how powerful it is. Jesus the Christ decided to do the same thing in his own way, for the reasons that made sense for those around him, whose DNA was working poorly.

There are energies within the Human Being that are catalysts to enlightenment. One of them is compassion, and you felt it this day, did you not? [speaking of the earlier presentation of the story of the 33 miners in Chile given by the teacher Jorge Bianchi] It touched your heart. So what would you say was the energy in the room, and what color was it, and how thick was it? Well, many of you would say there was no color at all. Some might ask, "*What do you mean by thick, Kryon?*"

As you sat there in the chairs, energy sat upon you and you felt your hearts squeezed a little bit. You had empathy for those who got their lives back, and you saw the hearts of relatives filled up to the point of weeping in joy. This is what I speak of – something invisible and yet "thick" with emotion. It is profound what you can create around you that will change lives in the room. Gaia knows you, and every compassionate moment is recorded.

Some of you have come for healing this weekend and I know this. So this would be a very good time to receive it. Those readings are no different, and perhaps you are in the chair for this reason also? There is an entourage here; there is compassion here; there is profundity of old souls here; this is a quantum soup of opportunity, dear one. Why don't you claim it right now – that you're going to rise from that chair of yours and have the seeds planted within you, by your own choice, for the health that you've asked for? Claim the beginning of the healing that you know has always been available, for you are starting to be in touch with the intelligence of your own Merkabah.

Spiritual organizations are filled with miracles. Hospitals are seeing documented results of that which is called *spontaneous remission*. This is where, suddenly, cellular structure does something that science cannot begin to explain. A total remission of disease occurs, sometimes almost overnight. But I'll tell you what it is: It's DNA temporarily going 100 percent for a moment and cleaning the body of dis-ease. You've seen it, but you just didn't know what it was.

So why don't you do it right now? If you can imagine it, then you can have it. See yourself with pure cellular health. It serves the earth, dear Human Being, for you to live longer than you think you're going to live. We need your light. So why not do it now?

Let all of those in the room join in compassionate consciousness right now in a quantum state that is entangled with all those here and reading, sending the compassion of healing to the ones who need it without even knowing their faces or their names. It's beautiful. Some day you'll see what the ceremony of Human Beings together can do when you all walk out healed! Why not? When you can go to a meeting for half a day and come out younger than you've been – why not? Then you'll start to see all of what I have said today is accurate and true. It is against all logic of prevailing scientific thought, but well within the purview of the love of God.

We leave this place and yet we don't. There'll never be a meeting like this again, with this exact number of souls, with the names that you have, with the Akash you have, so it's a unique meeting much as you are unique. Go from this place different than you came, and know that Kryon does not exist within the Human Being who is sitting on this stage.

Kryon exists in the quantum soup that is God. This *soup* is what walks out with you today if you choose.

If you choose.

And so it is.

I'll say it again: The old energy dies hard and it may be more difficult to see improvements in immediate times to come, because change is that way.

Lightworker, old soul, do not fear the changes that you have brought about. You have lived hundreds of lives to create this, and it's about time that this shift occurs. You are in the right life at the right time. Flow with it; understand it; celebrate it daily, and thank God that you're part of it, for it is the fruition of everything you've done and expected, and it's the very reason that Kryon is here. It is no wonder we wash your feet!

Ponder these things, for you have created them.

Kryon

The Recalibration of Self - Part One

Here we go. You just knew that with all this new energy talk, there would eventually be some admonitions about changing ourselves. In fact, it's the most important recalibration yet and it takes three chapters to discuss it. There is always some overlapping information, so expect a repeat or two of what you have already read. But it only makes sense that we must change the way see perceive things in order to make sense of what is coming. Here is Part One.

Lee Carroll

Chapter Nine
THE RECALIBRATION OF SELF - Part One
Newport News, Virginia
April 2012

Kryon
Book 13

Chapter Nine
The Recalibration of Self - Part One
Live Kryon Channelling - April 2012

Greetings, dear ones, I am Kryon of Magnetic Service. All the things that follow in this message today are about Human Beings and the things that are literally changing the paradigm of their reality. So the day has been filled with examples of thinking differently [speaking of the seminar], and this message will continue that theme. We have given you message after message since the first of this year indicating how things are different and asking you to look at something we are calling a "recalibration of all things".

I speak to you right now in a linear fashion with communication you are used to. This is possible due to the experience and practice that my partner has received over the years. He is intuitively able to translate this multi-dimensional communication from my side of the veil to yours.

Channelling is the process of translating spiritual messages through a Human Being. But in the process, you still have the Human Being's 3D filter in place. The culture, the language, the thought processes are all still there. Therefore, part of accurate channelling is for the channeller to learn to *step aside* and allow the information to flow with the least filtering possible. Channelling has never been a takeover of the Human's free will. That would be something you would call possession, and it is not that. Instead, it is a meld given in love to pass information, energy and communication from a loving source to you.

I tell you this because these lessons are difficult to communicate. If you have not experienced a certain kind of reality, then it is difficult for me to teach about it. You can't relate to it. Yet I do that today, knowing that it is difficult to understand. I give a message here in this chair that comes in three parts. Today's message is part one. Each message, however, is complete by itself. So this message will be complete unto itself and the others will be as well. But when you put these three together, they are greater than the sum of their parts. This is the third language at work, and there is more to this story than the words you are hearing.

If you have an open consciousness to these kinds of things, dear one, you'll already understand that your body recognizes what's going on. Young person, you're going to inherit a planet that is far different than the one your parents knew. The energy is changing and recalibrating. Many of you are starting to understand what is new before the Lightworker. I'll call this message, "The Recalibration of Self." This is not to be confused with "The Recalibration of Humanity," given before. This is the recalibration of your core being.

Energy – A Misunderstood Concept

Energy by itself is very difficult to define or explain. Often, when Humans talk about energy, they are referring to that which pulsates linearly through wires in a multi-phase system, such as your electricity. That's not what we're talking about. The energy we speak of is not singular information. It is not three-dimensional. Rather it is a multi-dimensional attribute all around you of a confluence of Earth and consciousness, and it brings about that which you call manifestation. You were born in a certain energy. We speak of the grids of the planet being in a certain energy, but it's not well defined. You may walk into a room and say, *"Well, the energy does not feel good in here today."* Another day you'll walk in and you'll say, *"Wow, did you feel the energy today?"* If someone pressed you to define this, you might have trouble. Yet you use the word to mean both positive and negative things, for you understand it's polarized.

What I'm about to speak about in this lesson refers to the *energy* that you are used to on the earth, whatever that means to you. It's the energy that you live in, work in, meditate in, and worship in – and this energy is changing. This affects what you consider to be *normal*, for it represents your comfort zone. So if we could give you any kind of energy advice, we would say, "Expect normal to change." That's hard to do.

The Human Being survives knowing where normal is supposed to reside and what it is supposed to feel like. When you walk from A to B, you expect certain things – the air you breathe, the gravity you experience, the magnetics that your cells are used to via the grid. What if I told you that many of those things won't be the same? But the only thing you are truly aware of as a Human Being is that *something is different.* Some of you may walk around saying, *"The energy feels odd today."* It's more than odd. It's recalibrating.

Changes in The Crystalline Grid – Changing the Past

Let us start by talking about the things that *feel* different to you. Here is an example of a recalibration, and it's a summary of what we gave you not long ago regarding the grids. We told you that the Crystalline Grid of this planet, an esoteric, invisible, multidimensional attribute of Gaia, was changing. We told you that it is the "action" memory of humanity. It remembers Humans and what they do. It's like the esoteric "memory grid" of Human action.

The Crystalline Grid is, therefore, linked to Gaia and responsible for that which you call portals, and also that which you call old, negative energy. It is profound in spots where war has been, for it reflects a memory of what Humans have done in battle. It reacts to Human emotion. That's the Crystalline Grid, and the metaphor of anything crystalline is that which holds memory and vibration. So imagine an invisible grid around the planet that remembers what Humans have done.

In places that feel dark, you may have had war upon war and battlefields that you would rather not walk into. Lightworkers often *feel* the misery of death, fear, and anxiety. This stays in the land, and you know I'm telling you something that many have experienced and told you about. There are also places on the grid that are portals of healing and joy, and what my partner even calls the womb of Gaia – a place where you can go and bathe in the thickness of Human compassion.

A little time ago, we told you something powerful about humanity. We told you that Human Beings are responsible for *posturing* or "loading" that planetary grid. However, as energy goes, it is typical that you would consider this system a *linear remembrance*. That is, you would think that both positive and negative things would be remembered and stored at the same level within the grid. But that's not the way it is, and you know all about this. What do you see on your news? What is the bias between joy and horror? This balance is Human nature, and the grid reflects that very attribute of humanism. It gives far greater emphasis to negative things.

Up to now, dear ones, the earth has remembered dark energy in a nonlinear way and has given greater emphasis to places where many have died and where there has been great suffering. The grid remembers the horror of battle a lot more than the birth of a child. It's responsible for what you call hauntings and ghosts and all those apparitions that are playing the tapes in the same way – that's the Crystalline Grid.

When you look at the planet and ask what vibration it is today, the measurement of the Crystalline Grid is used to answer that. That is what the vibration of the planet is based upon – what Humans are doing and have done in the past. Then we told you that the way the grid *remembers* Human action is starting to change.

So now you have an answer to a quantum question: *How can things done in the future change the past?* That is happening now, because what you are doing *now* is changing the linearity of the grid's "remembering system". So what happens is that positive is going to carry a far grander and greater energy to the grid. Therefore, it *overwrites* anything that was there, called past energy.

There'll be a day when you can walk into the battlefield and say, *"I feel nothing."* This is because there have been Humans who have trod this path who are Lightworkers and every step they took changed the attributes of the field they walked in. So the new energy is able to allow Humans who are alive now to rewrite the past!

Now, that's out of the purview of your reality. You're not with me on it. You want the storage process to be linear and it isn't. So we're saying there's a *recalibration of self* – that is to say, a recalibration of what you'd expect is real. It couldn't get any more personal than this. Imagine what the energy would be for humanity if the energy of history changed!

If the grid reflects Human consciousness and the grid is recalibrating, then the "self" of the Human is also recalibrating in the same manner. Human nature is following the model of what is taking place with the grid. humanity will eventually become softer, placing emphasis on beauty instead of horror.

Imagine a situation where oil does not float to the top when mixed with water. You might say, *"But oil always floats to the top. It has to. Because of its molecular bonding and density, it always floats to the top."* What if we said there'd come a day when physics itself may actually alter the reality of everything that you've known? What if the density of oil became closer to the density of water and, therefore, it would simply lie there in the middle and not float to the top? Now, if it did that, you would say, *"That's spooky. Something is wrong with this."* You wouldn't understand it, and that's the point.

Your reality biases you toward what has always been and does not allow for what might be.

If something could change to the degree that it upsets everything that you expected or thought was accurate and true, how would you react? Based upon your core survival experiences and what you've learned on the planet, how would you deal with it? Could you recalibrate yourself and say, *"I understand it used to be one way and now it's another,"* and move forward? Or would you look at it and say, *"I wonder when it's going to return to the way it was?"* This, dear ones, is the crux of this message, for as the energy on this planet shifts, even the old soul will be tempted to say, *"Sure, Kryon, it's wonderful. It's good. I love it. I'm going to work with it."* Then in their darkest hours, they're going to say, *"I'm tired of this! When will it return to the way it was?"* It's because you grew up in an energy where the duality was one way, but now it's starting to be another.

Recalibration of Self-Worth

Now we bring up the point of who the Lightworker is. The recalibration of self is going to be the recalibration of self-worth. Now, we've said it briefly before: the Lightworker is afraid of the dark. It's because the dark has beat you up every lifetime, hasn't it? Today we sit in a room of old souls who have come into this life yet again fearing what the dark energy might bring for them. But you came anyway, and you came in without knowing what was going to happen. There were many prophets who said you wouldn't make it past 2000. Now you are in 2012! Every time you arrive, the dark energy seems to be against you.

When I first arrived and presented myself to my partner, it was shortly after the Harmonic Convergence. I told my partner I was here because of what humanity had done. I told my partner I would not have been here otherwise, for there was nothing to teach, that you would not have made it. Does it make sense that I would arrive to teach you for 20 years then you all die horribly? No! I arrived because of the potentials of what are happening right now.

Those who were astute and who had felt the Kryon energy come into the planet knew why I had arrived. I represented an entire entourage coming to share the good news with old souls, to be their cheering section, because they had turned the energy of doom around. Against all odds, it had changed.

The Soviet Union had fallen over, a huge geopolitical event that had not been predicted anywhere! It disarmed the potential Armageddon of the planet. Other things started to move in directions that had no predictions anywhere in the past. There would have to be guidance and direction for this very day that you sit here. It would be a recalibration of your survival instinct and of what you think is real. This is the task for you now: are you able to cope with the recalibration or will you always be looking over your shoulder, wondering when the old "normal" is going to return?

The Story of the Old Soul

So this message is one of three, and it's an encouragement and an acknowledgment of who an old soul is and why this person needs to know what we have to tell them. So we will just *lay it out there* for you to see: The oldest souls in this room and hearing this have been through the worst of the worst. Every lifetime that is written upon your DNA's quantum Akashic memory carries engrams of emotion.

You came into the world expecting it to do what it always did. As soon as you started awakening to the truth that you carried in the past, you knew you might have to hide yet again. You might have blocked this from your memory, but it was there, embedded in the Akash. Some of you were burned at the stake not too far from here. Some of you came back and it all happened again! How many lifetimes does it take, shaman, before you sit and say, *"I'm not going to do this again"*?

You awakened in a modern society this time. Now you are a Lightworker, but you say, *"I'm going to go to the esoteric meetings, but I'm not going to tell others I'm going because I'm not going to go through that again."* You're careful who you tell about what you believe because you're tired of swimming upstream and having the current beat you back against the rocks. You're tired of losing family and friends or even jobs because you happen to believe that God is inside you. That is the story of the old soul who is here in the room and listening to these words.

The result of all this is an old soul who comes and stands tall as a Lightworker on Earth, but who also lacks self-worth. That's an oxymoron! How can you have a lighthouse that's uncertain of its own light or if it's doing anything worthwhile? Will the waves come and knock the light out? But that's who is in front of me and listening now, because you're all that way! You can't help it. Your past is your past.

This turnaround of energy on the planet cannot instantly create giants and heroes of self worth, especially among those who have practiced in the old energy for so many years. Perhaps you think you are ready for this shift? You are not – not for the energy that's coming. That's what we want to also address.

There is something coming where you will be able to manifest things only dreamed of, but it's going to take belief, realignment, and new understanding. You are going to have to start some basic survival perceptions that require you to understand that, dimensionally, you are more powerful in areas you cannot see than the ones you can. You weren't taught this in school or by your mother, and you have never practiced this. That's where you stand at this moment. *"Well then, what's going to happen, Kryon?"* The answer is that you're going to have to want to change. If you do not actively attempt to change, you will always be floating on the surface like the old oil.

The Darkness. Is It Alive?

Right now, you think you have an idea about how dark and light work on the planet. So let's bring this up in a way that you'll understand. Let's talk about dark and light attributes yet again. We have given you the information over and over that darkness is defined as the *absence of light*. Yet what do you do with this? In your spiritual mythology, you have decided that darkness must be intelligent. There has to be a consciousness behind darkness, you say, and because of this, there is a dark force with a name and, therefore, you fear it. You don't understand that physics demands that darkness can't exist in the light! Yet you still don't believe it. Darkness is a balance, not an entity.

Right now, there are Humans saying, *"Wait a minute, Kryon. Do you mean there's no such thing as evil?"* I didn't say that. Listen, Humans are powerful, and when Humans take that which has no light and they apply it to a consciousness of their own design, it becomes Human evil. Now, that has consciousness because a Human put it there. But alone, there is no entity out to capture your soul. Period. There is only a balance of dark and light. Humans are responsible for making darkness look like it has intelligence because manifestation works both positive and negative.

All of you are used to a certain balance on the earth. But it's not an intelligent balance. That's the first thing that you have to learn, Lightworker. There's no force against you! You don't believe it when you are told this. This is difficult for you, because you've always been taught there is something pushing against everything you do. Indeed, there is, but it is represented by Humans in the dark and not darkness with a personality.

The brighter your light, the less darkness can be around. *"Oh, Kryon, I love that. How can I make my light brighter?"* That's easy! It's by not fearing the dark! When you fear the dark, you give it your energy, don't you? So what is it you fear? It's survival, isn't it? For in the past, the darkness created by Humans has created turmoil in your life. Your very survival was at stake. Now that changes, and so does the dark/light balance.

There are so many things here, dear one, that you're going to have to recalibrate. Who are you trying to please, Lightworker? Let me ask you this: If you're trying to please God, you *are!* I wouldn't be here if you weren't. If you're trying to please those on the other side of the veil, who in some cases are your own parents looking back at you, you are! By the light that you have put here and by the light that you carry, all is well. Do you feel that? Or are you looking around for some other approval somewhere and not getting it? It's time for you to recalibrate these feelings.

I want you to understand something: God doesn't have Human emotions. God isn't sitting around hoping anything or wishing you would do this or that. God is the creative source of the Universe and you are part of this God. Therefore, to "please God" is to love yourself enough to be part of the wholeness of God. These are things you should know about the way you think and what is going to change.

"Kryon, do you mean there's not going to be a struggle since the newer energies are more benevolent?" Oh, dear one, there will be a struggle! This struggle between the dark and light balance on Earth is classic. You're going to watch it like a game played on your own ball fields, where the energies go back and forth and it doesn't seem to be one team winning or losing, just back and forth. When watching that, what will you think? In your heart of hearts, what are you going to say? *"Well, we've failed. Nothing is happening."* Indeed! That's because, dear ones, all you are willing to look at is the three-dimensional

game field. You're not looking at anything else that might be happening under it or above it. This is very hard to describe. This is the battle between dark and light.

How Can Darkness Battle Us?

"Well, Kryon, if darkness has no intelligence, how does it battle us?" Here are some attributes of the darkness that can explain it. Humans in the dark battle you. Darkness itself is just a balance.

Dark, negative energy is blind about what you're doing in the light. It's stupid about things of the light, and this is your advantage, for you can see everything and this energy of darkness can't. Humans walking in darkness, creating darkness with intent, can never compete with a Lightworker who can see everything. Integrity is blind to dark energy and will always win. Honesty and compassion and caring are always going to win over darkness. Benevolence and spiritual synchronicity are like full color in the black and white world of those who willingly walk in darker energy.

Now, it's simply an energy, like gravity is an energy, and like magnetism is an energy. When you see magnetism at work and you see things come together with force, do you look at them and give them names and assign consciousness to them? Do you think they are entities? No. Instead you say, *"This is physics. It's energy. It moves from here to there, like oil and water are also about physics. It's just energy. Oil floats because of its density. It's lighter than water's density."* Dark and light have these same kinds of attributes and darkness moves when light is present. It's not spooky, and it's not alive.

Here is the big difference: in the new energy, you are a light creator. Therefore, you are changing the density of the planet. Do you understand what I'm saying? Therefore, the balance of dark and light moves accordingly. It's not smart. It moves out of the way of the light. It moves out of the way of the Lightworker! Do you understand what I'm saying? For eons, this balance has not moved at all. Suddenly, it is moving out of your way as you walk toward it. It can't exist where you walk! It can't survive the way it used to and it will fight to keep it the way it used to be. But the balance will slowly change, and that's because you are not afraid of it.

Oh, dear Lightworker, this is the message of today's channel and also tomorrow's. I'm going to itemize some of the things that you will see regarding these changes. The one big item right now is this: What are you going to do with this new power? Although darkness is not intelligent, it is still a balancing force. Therefore, you can expect it to have an effect on everything as it changes. You can't have a rebalancing of such powerful influences on Human nature without change on both sides. Do you understand? Do not personalize darkness.

When you fall off a cliff, whom do you blame? Was it the gravity monster? What intelligence pushed you there and how dare it take you down and hurt you? This is an example of a force that is there, but understood for what it is.

Unlike gravity, dear ones, this particular balance on the planet is a multi-dimensional, elastic, dynamic thing. It has been the same way for eons and now it's not. It is moving accordingly to the energy that you have chosen to create. It is your fate. But unless you re-adjust to your power, nothing is going to happen.

The recalibration of self starts with understanding that darkness has no power over you anymore. It will retreat from you instead of attack you. If you fear anything, darkness has won. That's the balance we speak of. All this is difficult to explain since these things are going to occur in non-three-dimensional terms. My partner is even sitting here wondering if he has done a good job today. So I will say to him, "The job has been adequate."

The recalibration of the Lightworker is described as the Lightworkers discovering their real light, the light of the creator. They are discovering that it belongs there, that this is their time, and that they can turn it on. The darkness will have no chance of existing anywhere around them as long as they illuminate themselves with compassion and patience.

Let divinity shine through each of you as you walk on this planet and understand these things, for they are imminent.

Do you want to know why you came? This is why you came. It's not *to do*, but rather it's *to be*. It's to *be light* where darkness used to be. This is the message of the day. I am Kryon, in love with humanity.

And so it is.

Kryon

The Recalibration of Self - Part Two

Kryon continues his discussion of dark and light. This was covered in Chapter Five and also in Part One of the last chapter. The reason it is here again is because we give so much of our power away in the misunderstanding of it. It's also time to speak honestly about what we percieve as contracts, and also the amount of time we spend on conspiracies instead of ourselves. Kryon is starting to get to the very basics of our core, where fear and drama and old energy thinking keep us from our magnificence.

Lee Carroll

Chapter Ten
THE RECALIBRATION OF SELF - Part Two
Greensboro, North Carolina
April 2012

Kryon
Book 13

Chapter Ten
The Recalibration of Self - Part Two
Live Kryon Channelling - April 2012

Greetings, dear ones, I am Kryon of Magnetic Service. Tonight the message is about the recalibration of self, yet again. The message is one that asks the listener and the reader to go beyond what I call *survival* reality. Instead, we instruct you to move into the potential possibilities of things that are real, but which have no structural proof. What I mean by *structural proof* is that these things are not three-dimensional attributes that you understand. I'm asking this because that is what is required for recalibration of that which is personal, the very *core-self* that is you.

In review, I will say that the channel tonight continues the one from last night, but will be succinct within itself and complete. However, if you were to listen to both as a pair, it will be even more complete. Before we start, I will give a quick review of last night's information.

The Shifting Energy of Recalibration

The energy on the planet is what is shifting, but you cannot really define it as energy as you know it. We said before, if we ask you what energy is, most would see it in a wire as electricity or in a place that *feels* a certain way. You do not think of energy as being that which emanates from a Human Being on a regular basis. The idea that the Human is transmitting and receiving certain kinds of multi-dimensional energies all the time is not something that you were taught when you were a child. To come into that realization is inviting many to think that you are odd, spooky and weird. This is because you cannot assign any kind of recognizable, validated attribute to it that is consistent and constant. Therefore, it is outside of the purview of what you would call *that which makes sense,* formulated and empirical [verifiable]. So how are you going to use something that you don't understand even exists? It's difficult, yet that is what we are asking you to do.

In addition, you have those things that restrict your belief or that are connected to Human bias. You are based in tradition and often in mythology [things that you have been taught are a certain way]. One of these is what we spoke of last night. We asked you about your perception of dark and light. Then we encouraged you to understand that darkness by itself has no intelligence. We know you assign intelligence to all of these kinds of things because it is your tradition to do so, and it makes it simple. When you feel resistance, you assign an entity to it, not an understanding that it might simply be energy that is working a certain way.

A Review of Dark and Light

Again, we define light and dark. We continue to tell you that light has an active attribute and darkness does not. Therefore, darkness must be defined as *the absence of light.* But the balance between the two is, indeed, something you can understand. If we told you there was going to be a new balance of dark and light, you'd say, *"I understand that."* If I told you that light was going to change and darkness was going to change, you'd say, *"What does that mean?"* Is evil going to change? Are there more angles coming? Human Being, why are you so adamant about assigning personal attributes to physics? If you put your hand in an invisible place and you feel something push back, chills would run down your spine and you'd say, *"Who is that?"* That's funny! Let me ask you something. When you jump up in the air and gravity pushes you down, do you get chills down your back and say, *"Who is that?"* Are you afraid? No. You know better, because you grew up with gravity, and it's the biggest *pusher* of all! You didn't assign an entity to it, did you?

When you work with magnetics in a laboratory, and you are working with the power of the positive and the negative in repelling and pushing, you get to see wonderful invisible energy. So, have you assigned names to all that? No. Only ignorant Humans in the past might have done that, without understanding. They haven't grown up with magnets that push and pull on each other. For the scientists among you, what you are seeing in the laboratory at the atomic level are atoms that are simply missing some parts. Those atoms that are missing their parts are looking for other atoms that *have* those parts! They're constantly attracted and repelled through a process of unequal energy trying to balance itself. This is physics. It's energy, and these atoms will always seek to find an atomic structure that has the parts they want or repel the ones that are not candidates. It's about balance. That's magnetism.

And I'm going to tell you the truth, dear ones. There's no negative entity that tries to push you around in life with horns and a tail! Yet there are things that push and pull that you cannot see, and you want to believe they are alive. Enter the truth about dark and light: These are attributes of Human consciousness and physics working together to create a system that affects you. But there is no "dark entity after you soul".

Dark Entities

"Kryon, I can't believe there is no such thing as dark entities. Really?" Let's set the record straight in this enhanced channelling. I have actually mentioned in the past years that there are dark entities. Yes, there are. However, first I want you to understand that Humans have a tendency to personalize and fear anything that is dark. I want you to start using your spiritual logic and discern what is what. Your tradition and your mythology are strong, and they bias you in this direction. So you tend to fear everything in the dark instead of realizing the truths that are there. That's what this discussion is about, and the channelling before this one.

The dark entities of the planet are real. But they have consciousness behind them and not simple physics. So you must know that there are Humans who have voided themselves of light so completely that they themselves are dark entities. They use this "power of darkness" to enslave other Humans in fear. So they are dark entities, and this is their choice. They are often powerful, since they exude a consciousness of evil. You have seen them in your history and seen how humanity often "buys into" their power. This is an old energy where evil breeds on itself as it continues to wipe out any light it sees anywhere around it.

There are also dark entities who are not Human that come and go on a regular basis. These are conscious beings that visit you and try to frighten you to see how you are going to react. There is a constant test at hand on how Human consciousness is evolving, and the very fact that almost everything you see in physics has a polarity about it should tell you that so do dark and light consciousness. But as we have discussed many times, these who would come from other places in the Universe have no power over you unless you allow them to. They have no "God inside" and are simply "intelligent biology". Their entire fascination with you is that you *do* have "God inside", and they just can't figure it out! So they have found that fear is the key to contain you while they examine anything they wish to.

By holding your light high, no dark entity from anywhere can touch you. They will see your light and walk the other way. Their very existence depends on weaker Humans who see their power and want to be part of it. For you, the admonition is as it always was: Claim the love of God in your life and recognize that you are part of the creative source. Your Higher-Self is unique in the galaxy and no other life has it. On this Earth, you do, and it is currently the only planet of free spiritual choice because of that. You *are* light.

The Crystalline Grid

Multi-dimensional attributes within systems on the planet balance much like magnetics, and they are always in play. One of the attributes that we told you was changing was one of the most esoteric of all, and that is the Crystalline Grid. At the moment, the Crystalline Grid does not *remember* things linearly. If things happen that are negative, it remembers them first, since it *sees* them with a higher power quotient than things that are positive. So therefore, when you walk on former battlefields, you feel it profoundly. Negative actions are treated with a higher value than positive. That's going to change.

As the energy shifts with Human consciousness as the catalyst, the Crystalline Grid remembrances shift. It did in the past as well. So what you do today rewrites how the Crystalline Grid remembered it yesterday. Let's say that what you do today tends to erase or cover up some of the energy as remembered in the past. So here you are with the axiom that I've given you before: What you do in the future changes the past! For the Crystalline Grid is becoming less linear than it used to be and is going to start remembering things far differently than it used to. A sensitive Lightworker standing on a battlefield in the near future won't *feel* what happened in battle near as much. We told you to expect this. Your thoughts today are rewriting the self-worth that the Crystalline Grid remembers, and it's a hard adjustment.

Last night, we left with this: We wanted you to understand more about the push/pull energy of dark and light and what may very well happen next. Try your very best – without assigning a personality or entity to it. Darkness is stupid. It has no intelligence. It is simply part of a system that wants to survive for balance, just like so many other systems on the planet. The ones at the atomic level are designed to balance, and it looks like survival since it's constant and eternal.

The Final Battle

When you start to actually rewrite the attributes of the system, dark and light start to change their balance also. So what I'm trying to tell you, Lightworker, is that *dark* is going to resist and start to push back harder for balance and survival. But since it is not empirical science, and is instead consciousness, there are some things you don't expect about it all. You can control the dark energy as it starts to push to balance itself back to where it used to be. So I will tell you yet again, something that many still don't understand: If you're part of the light, you can *trick* the dark because you can see and it cannot! That is the secret, dear one, yet the dark is still going to come forward in a multi-dimensional way to try to snuff out the light. This is the battle of the shift, and even represents the way physics works in the entire universe – push and pull.

For the first time in Human history, Lightworkers have the clear advantage, for Gaia is tuned to what you are doing. You are passing the marker of the precession of the equinoxes and moving into a place where the very balance of the planet is changing, and it is with you, not against you. You're about to plant seeds of peace on Earth, and in the process, an old balance of light and dark will be interrupted. Eventually, like some of the other planets we have discussed, the dark will diminish to a place where there will be no more war. Countries will continue to have disagreements, but the solutions will never be to kill another Human. It will slowly disappear from the options that humanity would consider. There will simply be no more war.

We have told you that someday you will look back on the time before 2012 and see it as a demarcation point. You will say, *"Humans were barbaric in those days. We are a different race today."* That's how different it has the potential to be. Do you think basic Human nature can change that much? That's the issue before you. It's that profound.

We talked about the bridge of swords. We talked about a battle that is coming, and this is it. You're in it. The swords are a metaphor for *celebration*. You are beginning to walk under a bridge of swords, as you have seen during marriages and celebrations in military victory. Spirit puts them there for you to feel and crosses them above your heads and you walk underneath them. Lightworker, on your way to the battlefield, you have already won! It begins with a realignment of self, but it isn't going to be easy.

The New Information

Let us describe in this short time what we did not talk about yesterday. Let us itemize some of the things that basic dark energy, starting to be out of balance, will bring to you to look at. If you can see these things, you will know it's coming and you can conquer it easier.

Now, remember there is no intelligence with basic darkness. So again, as we cover these things, think of gravity and other attributes of chemistry and physics that move to create balance. Think about oil and water. What if the oil changed weight? There would be a new battle to rebalance many mixtures. So with that in mind, how do you think the energy of darkness would react to try and rebalance your light? Now, although it is not intelligent, it moves as though it is. If it's used to a certain balance, and your light increases, it's going to react.

Darkness by itself is innate, but it is reactive to balance. However, dark energy with the help of a Human Being's consciousness is evil. So remember the above discussion about dark entities? The basic attribute of balance on the planet has no intelligence of its own, but the new balance is beginning to be seen by those of low consciousness. It works both ways, dear ones. Think about "darkworkers" as being the opposite of Lightworkers. They are out there, and it helps to explain the power of those processes where

Human Beings can conjure up that which seems to be demonic. It gives credibility to that which is voodoo and will easily marry to a belief system of those who are afraid of it. Humans give power to darkness by fearing it. It you feed it with fear, it becomes stronger. So this is complex, but that's why we are teaching it.

Although you're not fighting an entity that is dark, in a way you are fighting the energy generated by other Humans who are "collecting the dark". Now, you expected that, did you not? There will be an element of Human nature that will fight the light, but remember, this element is still in the dark and can't *see* what you can. What do you think that dark energy will do to try and balance what is happening and quench your light? Let's study it.

Fear is The Greatest Tool of The Dark

Light is diminished, if not extinguished totally, by fear. If there's anything the darkness knows with the help of intelligent Human Beings, it is that if you are afraid, it has already won. In physics, in nature and all through the planet, current balance resists change. If change is inevitable, there are certain things within the system that will fight to the death to keep things the same. This is what you are facing in 2013 and beyond. It's an old paradigm and old balance of humanism that will try to remain the same. In Human terms, sometimes it will be greed, power and a comfort with the way things used to be. All of that is eventually going away, but the darkness is almost like a reservoir for those who wish to create the old balance to survive, but they will not win. You are the Lightworker planting the seeds. Here is what to expect.

If they can make you afraid, they will. Now, those who are listening, those who are reading and those in the room, you might say, *"I am not afraid, Kryon. I have the love of God in my heart. I am not afraid. I am not even afraid to die. I know about the circle of life, I know about the love of God, and I am not afraid."* But here is what

I'm going to tell you, dear one: You might be. Because the dark, with the aid of other Human Beings, knows about your *Achilles' heel*, Lightworker. What would you be afraid of, really?

I will say it again. Lightworkers have an attribute that is counterintuitive to what you would expect. It's lack of self-worth. You've been beaten up! I've said it before. I said it last night. Many of you have come into this planet not even knowing what was going to happen this time. Oh, the potential was there that you would come to this marker and move past it, but it was not a certainty. What if it was like all the other times you came? How many lifetimes did other Humans make you a sacrifice to their mythology because you were strange or had power or could see colors, or worse, you could heal people? How has that affected you at the core level?

So here you are now. You come into this lifetime powerful in light and weak in self-worth, and you know it. So again, what is it you would be afraid of? I'll tell you.

Number one – are you really correct about all this esoteric New Age talk? Is this really happening or are you just a gullible, nice person who has grasped on to the lunatic fringe and spiritual emptiness of the New Age? Have you lived your life in naivety and foolishness? Ask some of your relatives! They will give you a resounding YES! But you might say, *"I am not afraid that I might be wrong. I know I am right. I feel it in my heart. I have the love of God and the wisdom of the ages."* So I'm going to tell you that there will be things that will make you question yourself. There is always that persistent *seed of doubt* that lasts and lasts, until you are on your deathbed. Even then, you'll never know. Do you see where I'm going with this, dear ones? Lightworkers are the worst when it comes to holding the faith. They are easy to beat up.

This darkness, which is not intelligent, tries to balance light and dark. Like atomic structure, it knows what to do. Darkness knows what you're afraid of. Now, the irony here is that it also doesn't know much about light – only about itself. It can't even see you. So you can dance around it and move around it. But it can make you afraid. It can lead you to a place where deep down you wonder if you have it right. Darkness knows how to create doubt. It's a specialist.

Dear one, let's look at your bias. You were trained in a three-dimensional world with three-dimensional spirituality, and your leaders told you over and over, *"If you don't do this right, you're going to fail. You won't please God. You might even lose your soul."* It also may occur to you that maybe, just maybe, you've been doing it wrong! And in doing it wrong, you've displeased God, or worse. You're not fulfilling the purpose that you came for. After all, if you were, wouldn't things be going better in your life?

Let's say somebody comes along who looks like a Lightworker and who tells you you've failed and haven't pleased God. *"You're not fulfilling your contract. You've believed wrong things, and you are alone, without God, because of it."* You will hear these false prophets and they will appear to be one thing, yet they are not. They'll be true representatives of the dark, who appear to have the light. This is the war that we spoke of. It's the war of belief, and it knows how you think.

Light and dark are clashing in a multi-dimensional way in a back-and-forth manner that you didn't expect, and the issue for you isn't just *being afraid.* Dark will trick you if you allow it to. Dark will come along and say, *"Well, have you found your life's purpose yet?"* Most of the Lightworkers in the room will say, *"Not really. But I know I will someday."* And the darkness will say, *"You're a fool! It's too late. You followed the wrong person, meditated incorrectly, and as proof, nothing in your life is working. You've failed God and you've failed yourself. Come follow me now."* This sounds way too simple a trick, doesn't it, dear ones? However, the answer is that the old soul will be the first to fall for this! Darkness is so 3D, and it knows that you are tired and these are trying times.

I want you to watch for this, dear ones, for this is how you're going to know what dark is and what it's not. If darkness tells you, *"You've failed!"*, this information is not correct and is not of the light. Would Spirit do this? No. If anyone on this planet stands in front of you and says, *"You haven't found your contract!"* or *"When are you going to get with it spiritually?"*, that is not coming from the light.

I give you the truth, and the truth is something I have given over and over. Lightworkers are here to stand and show their light, not to *do* things. You were born on the planet to walk from A to B, to have compassion for other Human Beings, and to show the family what love is. Your purpose on the planet is to be an example to others around you of how love works, to be gentle in your countenance, and to act like a master. You are not here to write a book or build a healing center or do any of the other things that you've been told you *should* be doing. Did you hear me? *Being here* is what you came for. We celebrate your light! As long as you walk on the earth and understand this, darkness cannot touch you, for you won't be afraid of an obvious false message. You made the rules, dear ones. Don't let anyone now tell you what the rules are. You know them because they are etched on your heart by the love of God.

Contracts

Let me give you a concept if you haven't heard it before: If you want to have a contract, fine. If you've been told that you have a contract here on the planet, fine. But it's in invisible ink! *"What?"* you ask. *"No it isn't, because I wrote it and I remember what it's supposed to be."* Well, dear one, let me give you some news. Your *contract* is based on a starting energy when you get here, and it sits there ready to be rewritten every day! How about that? If you came to the planet with a contract regarding your life, your Akash and your path, what do you think happens when the whole planet shifts? Same contract? No. This system is designed so it can be changed all the time. Your only contract is to *be here* and create synchronicity with others. As you do, your contract and purpose change. What a great system! It actually knows what you are doing!

The dark loves this subject, and it's going to come in cloaked and say, *"What are you doing with any abundance? You had a contract to come in and suffer like all the other prophets and masters did. Don't you know that? Things may look better for awhile, but eventually you're going to be swatted down again, because Humans who love God must suffer."* Has anybody told you that? Yes! So I want to say, "Meet the darkness!" For this is the battle, having others define you. Your self-worth is your Achilles' heel, old soul. What are you going to do about it?

The Ways of Change

Briefly, I would like to tell you some things that may happen that are going to make you afraid or make you doubt your information. The potentials are afoot for the darkness to work this puzzle in ways you might not expect. Just when you think you are working for a better peace on the planet, there may be a small war. If this potential happens, what are you going to do with that? Are you going to throw up your hands and say, *"I knew I was wrong! Darkness won, and things are no different than they ever were."* Or, are you going to look at it and say, *"I see the deception. Humans are simply reacting to the shift and fighting the dark energy. It's not going to last long."* Let me tell you something else you should know: The younger people of this earth do not want war. They do not want war anywhere, and they don't want their father's wars to continue. If war occurs, it's going to be the elders who tell them it's the only way to get the changes they want. Again, the darkness does what it can to disguise itself as appropriate.

In the meantime, you're going to look at it and say, *"What's happening? I thought things were going to get better."* Listen, what is one of the worst things that could take place that would make you doubt that the planet is changing? I will tell you what to look forward to and what to expect. It's something you didn't think could happen – a split in the New Age. You may have to make a decision, or not.

I encourage you not to participate in a split of any kind. If you have a consciousness that has no boxes to get in or out of, then how can it split? If you have a consciousness where there is no membership or doctrine, then how can it split? Yet there will be those who say, *"Well, the processes and energies are always the same, but you're not doing the right thing. Therefore, we cast you away unless you change. You cannot be a Lightworker in our eyes."* Welcome to the old ways, where Human Beings always take divine attributes, put their own spin on it, and climb into their own box and call you *wrong*. What are you going to do with that in your own backyard, done by people perhaps you love? How do you deal with that?

Holding Your Own Energy

Try this solution: *"Woo hoo! I get to continue on my path without the drama of the others in my life. I'm free! Bless all of you for your search for truth. My love is with you as you go your way. Meanwhile, I'll be right here holding my light as I always have. My focus is the God inside, and it's all I need."*

Capture that which is the love of God within you and don't let go! Don't let the intellect trick you into thinking you've got to go one way or the other. If you hold a master's energy, then nothing can touch you. Let the others go and spin in their own drama. Meanwhile, you're going to plant the seeds of the new energy on the planet. That's why you came.

Conspiracies

There'll be conspiracy talk, and the subjects will be believable and ugly. Darkness loves this, and conspiracies are the tool of the dark. They function well because nobody knows if the information is real or not and that's what dark energy counts on. These will be conspiracy theories you haven't even heard of before, and there will be a lot of them. Recognize them when they show up. Know that they are not from the light and realize they are not accurate. Recognize them and cast them away, and do not make them part of your reality. The whole purpose of them is to make you doubt that you have passed the marker of 2012 into a new reality. They will try to convince you that nothing has changed.

It's not necessary to argue with those who come forward with these ideas. Instead, your job is to see the love of God in your life and also recognize it in them as well. That's all you have to see. Leave the information alone and move forward planting the seeds of light on the earth. Can you imagine what the masters of the planet went through? Who confronted them, and with what, and what they did with it? Nothing! Did you read where they argued or had discussions on who was right? They didn't have to. They were above it, all of it. They moved forward and put their light where it needed to be.

You Have the Upper Hand

This is not a frightening message, and the reason is because the old balance of darkness doesn't have a chance. I tell you these things mainly for those who are reading and listening in other places beyond this one. There are many who may not have that which the old soul has, which is the wisdom of the multiplicity of lifetimes placed upon you, such as those in this room. Those here in the chairs know better. Some of you have fought the battle already and know exactly what I speak of. Look for these things that

I have given you today as proof that what I bring you is true and real. The potentials are there and darkness doesn't have a chance to prevail again.

The Humans who are invested in the darkness as their reality will realize after awhile that the old ways don't work anymore. Watch for this as well. There will be those who try to recreate race war. But what might have worked 40 or 50 years ago is going to fall on its face because fewer will join in this than before. Old leaders be shocked that so few wish to cooperate. There will be a new silent consensus that says that the old issues, although still there, can't be solved with more violence. Those who are interested in creating things from the past that worked so often for them – things that are negative and ugly – will find that they just won't work any longer.

Terrorism: There'll come a day, dear ones, when the few terrorists who are left will not be able to recruit anyone for their causes. Slowly, there will be an acknowledgment even within their own circles that terrorism doesn't work anymore. And slowly, the Humans who would then use the dark in this way will pass. Darkness is truly stupid, linear and only reactive to imbalance. Slowly, you'll see a planet that changes consciousness, and the seeds that you planted with the love and compassion of God will bloom and grow. And yes, you'll be here to see it! Although, you may consider this statement a Kryon joke, all of you are scheduled for return. All of you, everyone in the room.

Your Return

I speak to those in the room. After you left the last time, you could hardly wait to get back. You knew of the potentials of what has now happened and you came back as fast as possible to work the puzzle. Now, you are poised at a new beginning, yet some of you are saying that you're tired and the battle is won. Hardly! Let me ask you something: After this current life, after planting these sacred seeds for lifetimes, are you going to walk away and wonder whether they will ever grow? Is that what you're going to do? Are you going to go through all this trouble – hundreds of lifetimes – to get to this place where the energy is cooperating with you and the fields are planted, then you walk away? I think not! Your next incarnation has such promise!

You're not going to have to go through what you did before. You're not going to come in spiritually stupid and then have to discover everything again that you did in this lifetime. As a young child, shortly after you realize who you are, you're going to have intuitive remembrance of a compassionate way of living.

What I'm telling you is that when you come back, dear ones, it's not going to be the way it was this time. All of the knowledge you learned this time will be available instantly within your free choice to awaken, and you will walk a wise path even before you're 20. Wouldn't you like that? You won't make the same mistakes. You're not going to have to wallow through partnerships that don't work or other challenges that have taken their toll on you. Instead, you will come in with an intuitive "knowing" of what works.

Then I'll tell you what you're going to be looking for when you're old enough. Everywhere you go, you'll be looking for the results of the seeds that you planted. You'll want to check them out. I'm not going to explain that. It's just to say that you'll know that they're growing and that the earth will be a little lighter because of it. There will be more compassion in society and a softer planet.

Dear ones, there will come a time when you'll look at it all and say, *"We did this."* Your self-worth will soar in a way that's appropriate – not the ego, but the God-Self within you – and you will say, "It is well with this planet." And then you'll know why you're here.

I'm Kryon, in love with humanity. And so it is.

Human Beings believe that their brains are capable of any thought that is thinkable in the Universe, and that the sky is the limit. They believe that at any given time, any intellectual can come up with whatever is needed. This would create the next step in evolved thinking. Yet history doesn't show that, does it? The fact is that invention and science are given to you when you are ready. You cannot "think" your way past this spiritual attribute.

In the past, we have brought up the fact that it should have been obvious to you centuries ago, how to fly and glide in man-made vehicles. Now, of course, you have discovered it. As we speak, thousands of Human Beings are in the air, flying from one place to another using principles that the birds showed you thousands of years ago. Yet it's new to humanity, having only been developed recently. Now, how long have you been looking at birds and longing to fly? How long have certain cultures been flying kites? Yet you never figured it out! How's that for being a Human Being with unlimited intellecual abilities?

Dear ones, the compassion of the masters has also been here for thousands of years, but now you are seeing it, and the energy is right. Now it's time to fly!

Kryon

The Recalibration of Self - Part Three

Kryon finishes this triology of the *recalibration of self* by going through some of the basic Human emotions and talking about each one. He invites us to get out of our box of old thought and into a place where our perception includes *"the God inside."*

Lee Carroll

Chapter Eleven
THE RECALIBRATION OF SELF - Part Three
Indianapolis, Indiana
July 2012
Kryon
Book 13

Chapter Eleven
The Recalibration of Self - Part Three
Live Kryon Channelling - July 2012

Greetings, dear ones, I am Kryon of Magnetic Service. The clock as you know it does not exist on my side of the veil, and your reality is not mine. I sometimes speak of things that are in your future and are showing themselves based upon the strongest potentials of humanity. That's what we report to you and that is what this message is about today – the ability of humanity to change. Whoever you are reading this, we have a bond you might not realize. This bond comes from the number of lifetimes you have had on this planet and the very core soul that you have and that is my friend. This friendship is the strongest when you are not pretending to be a Human.

Long before there were planets and galaxies, we romped together in the Universe, you and I. It's difficult to explain things that are beyond explaining, for the attribute of The Creative Source is *that which is and always was.* Our reality is a circle and, therefore, has no beginning or end. *Time* is an attribute that is placed upon your reality for a corporeal Human Being who must exist in four dimensions right now. This is why sometimes you look at everything around you and your intellect will ask time questions such as, *"When did it happen? When will it happen? Where will I be?"* Believe it or not, none of those questions make sense on my side of the veil. Your core soul was around long before you ever got here on this Gaia planet. Your legacy is huge, and right now the one you are creating with your imprint will be felt in this galaxy for all time. Not long ago, all of these things were only potentials, even as I sat before you 22 years ago and said for the first time, *"Greetings, dear ones, I am Kryon of Magnetic Service."* Much has happened since then and now many potentials have manifested. So we get down to the basics.

Getting Out of Your Box

In the lectures my partner describes things that are outside of your reality and, therefore, hard to conceptualize. He does this to help you get ready for a realization that you must push the envelope of what you truly think is real to enter the next phase of your lives. By pushing that envelope of belief, there is the possibility of expanding elements of your personal abilities that you don't even know you have. This is all very clear to us, but it's still a mystery to you. This mystery starts to clear, however, as you push the limits of your *room of reality*. All of these metaphors mean that at some level, Human Being, you have to sit with yourself and analyze honestly what you believe about yourself.

We must bring up difficult subjects that are often personal. The title of this channelling is similar to some that we've given before. In this third part of the "Recalibration of Self" series we begin to ask some of the most basic questions of your survival in the future. Are you going to be able to move forward? Is there anything stopping you? Are there are any blocks to your progress? How do you know what to do?

The Preparation: Self-Examination

Here is the premise: Like everything else that you have ever done in your life, there has to be some acknowledgment of the issue and then preparation. Can you begin to *mine the Akash* as we have told you? Yes. Can you start pulling in things for yourself that would slow your aging? Yes. Can you start actually changing your life in a way where you might start recreating yourself as a peaceful Human Being where perhaps there isn't one now? Yes. Can you pull in solutions to problems that you don't think are solvable? Yes. But you're going to have to prepare.

Now we get to the hard part. You are going to have to start taking stock, as they say, of who you are. You must look carefully and honestly at some old energy basics and ask yourself the difficult questions. We've got a list, of course, and it's five elements deep. Are you ready? You may sit there and say, *"Yes, I am."* But I might reply and say, "Perhaps not," for you are about to assimilate some of the attributes that have been taught by the masters of the planet. This is not all that difficult, dear one, unless your *reality box* won't allow it. It starts with understanding, recognition, belief and intent.

What Are You Afraid Of?

Number one –**Fear.** What are you afraid of? You might say, *"I'm not afraid of anything about my spirituality. I'm ready to go!"* Really? I want to tell you something: You're afraid of many things that you are not acknowledging. Some of them are buried deep and hidden in that elusive Akash of yours and it affects you every day of your life. It's why so many of you are dysfunctional in so many ways. You carry around things from the past that have etched themselves into a place in your behavior, which then makes you *go the other way* when you see something coming you don't like. That's fear. Now, it may not be on top of your 3D fear list, but it's a fear. So that's the first thing. What is it that changes what you might do or where you might not go? You might answer, *"Well wait a minute, Kryon. Some things might be there, but it's not my fault."* Wait. I'll get to that.

Ego

Number two – ego. *"Well, Kryon, you don't have to worry about that. I settled that years ago. My ego is balanced. I'm a Lightworker, and I know about ego."* Really? Let me ask you something. When you're with other Lightworkers, what do you talk about? Do you sit and listen and revel in the beauty of what they have to say, or do you talk about what you're doing and how you are helping the planet? Do you talk about how you have worked on yourself and all about your processes? That's a form of ego, dear one, in case you didn't know it. Perhaps you're proud of how much you've accom-

plished in the metaphysical processing of yourself . Let me give
you a secret. If you have really done the work on yourself, you never
have to tell a soul! They will see it in your wisdom and quiet silence.
So I'll give you an exercise. The next time you go for a meal with
friends, here is your task: Don't say anything about yourself. Zero,
unless you are asked. This is going to tell you what your habits are
and if your ego is "disguised in lightwork." This task will reveal if
you have a habit that you didn't realize. Again, I ask you: Did the
masters of Earth do this? When they gathered around with others,
did you hear them talk about themselves and how much they had
done? The answer is no. They sat at the feet of those who came to
see them and they listened and they talked about the beauty of the
Great Central Source and fed those around them with gracious
wisdom and love.

Anger

Number three – anger. What about anger? How are you in
that department? Perhaps you'll say, *"Well, I don't often get angry."* I
didn't ask you when. What do you get angry at and why? What's
the trigger, and why is it there? Every Human has triggers.

So, again, what was the trigger for the masters? The answer is
that they didn't have any. Not really. Instead, they had disappointment. If you ever saw a master seemingly angry, it was frustration
and disappointment with situations. The things that disappointed
them were the things that disappoint the God inside all of you
– war, cruelty to other living things, inhumanity between people,
lack of willingness to see love, and the imbalance created by fear.
So what makes you angry? If you've got anything that will always
make you angry, then you've got something to work on, don't you?
You might say, *"Well, wait a minute, Kryon, you see, this is not my
fault."* Wait. I'll get to that.

Reactive Action

Number four – reaction. What do you react to? What is it you can hardly wait to pop in and give your opinion about? Perhaps it's political? Somebody is saying something that is really off track. You know better so you've got to correct them. What triggers you? I'm not talking about anger. I'm speaking about reaction to a stimulus.

One very common reaction is *defense*. If somebody says something about you and it's blatantly not true, what do you do? Perhaps it's due to their ignorance or their misunderstanding, but how do you react? Do you quickly want to set them straight? Do you want to give them the facts, perhaps, so they will know better? Again, I ask you, how much of that defensive attitude did you see in the masters who walked this planet, dear one? When accused, did you see them fly off the handle and give a lecture in their defense? The answer is no. There were no triggers and there were no reactions. Did you notice? The masters were at complete and total peace with themselves. *"Well, wait a minute. That's not my fault. You see, Kryon, because..."* Wait. I'll get to that.

Judgment

Number five – judgment. Are you in judgment of anyone or anything? When you view others, what's the first thing you see? You might say, *"I'm not a judgmental person."* I didn't ask you that. What do you see? What did the masters see when they looked at another? They saw *God inside*. That's the first thing they saw. No matter what the situation was and no matter where they were, they only saw the larger picture. If somebody cuts you off on the roadway, do you see the God inside them or do you have a judgment of their character or actions that would define their consciousness in an inappropriate way? Do you see what I'm saying? What's your trigger, dear one? *"Kryon, you have to listen. You can't just throw what the masters did to those of us who are just regular Humans. It's not fair. We have some differences..."* I'll let you talk next.

The Human Responds

Now I'll let the Human Being talk. Tell me what you think about this discussion.

"Kryon, you don't understand. I came in with these attributes and I've been trying to unlearn them all my life. And, yes, I know it – sometimes I'm judgmental and sometimes I get angry and sometimes I react. I can't help my politics, it's what my parents taught me and it's ingrained in my mind. I can't help the fact that I do certain things the way I do them because that's who I am. Yes, I know there are some triggers. But, Kryon, I'm a Human Being and not really a master. So give me a break. These are all normal Human attributes. We can't help it. We come in with them and even Lightworkers have some of these issues."

A New Reality to Consider

Ah, dear Human, you are correct in your perception, but you don't have all the information yet. You only have the tradition of your learned reality. So allow me to give you some good information that you didn't expect. All of you come in with engrams, or templates, of how you react and behave. However, these are all "holdover Human attributes" that beg to be changed. They beg to be changed! Every single excuse that you will give cannot be accepted, since a truth exists that you didn't expect.

Here's a new concept: All the attributes I have given above, which you wish to tell me are simply Human nature, are not! They are a starting template of basic personality traits that are old, and they lie there ready to be altered! The masters will look at what you have said and they will say, *"You don't have to have these things. Why don't you get rid of them? Don't you understand that this is what we showed you how to do when we walked the earth? This is why we came as Humans like you."*

You make an interesting linear assumption, dear one, that what seems to make up your Human personality is something you came in with that is cemented there forever. It's YOU and you have to live with it and work on it forever. You paste it upon your persona and that's the way it is. This is your traditional thought, and you see each Human as having permanent personality attributes. This is not true.

What I am telling you is that every single item in the list of five, which we're going to go through again in a minute, has been given to you *to alter*. The alteration of these attributes is the recalibration of your basic personality that will take you right into multi-dimensional thinking and move your life towards balance and the things you really want. As you rewrite these personality templates, you can move forward in all the things we've been teaching. If you don't clear the way, it's going to be harder for you in the future.

Psychiatrists and psychologists – God bless these Human Beings, for they work with others to try and help them in their lives with balance. They are dedicated to it and passionate about it. The interesting thing about psychologists and psychiatrists is that many of them started as unbalanced and that's what brought them to work on solving the puzzle to help humanity. They see it in themselves, so they know what it feels like. They study it. They work with it and they teach it. But if you ask them how they do it, they will say they work with Human nature, a static model of Human behavior that is a science. Using this static model, they try to repair it through the Human's conscious awareness, through realization, practice and repetition. Sometimes it's a 12-step program, getting rid of addictions, fears, habits and more. But this science is all centered around a model that is permanently there and one that they can't alter. It's "Human nature" and the premise is that the static model can never change. It can be understood and covered up and tricked, but it can't be changed. And that, my dear Human Being, is the difference between a linear Human model and a quantum one. For now we tell you that you don't have to work on your fears or impulses. You can simply rewrite them.

Now we will go through the list yet again. Everything that has occurred in your life is rewritable. You cannot change the past, but you can change how you react to it. The very things that you would use as an excuse for why you do things the way you do will then belong to another Human – the one you used to be, not the current *you*. You will start to rewrite the actual engrams of your personality traits that more aptly represent the masters of history. You're going to find that as you begin, it won't be that hard, and it's self-balancing.

FEAR: What are you afraid of? All of your subconscious fears are based upon past-life experiences. This can be seen as just "data" that you carry around that was written a long time ago and is still active. What do you avoid? What is it that you do not want to do because of some energy you can't explain? All of these things, some of them unexplainable to you, can be cleared by rewriting them. They are not being covered up. They are being rewritten. The Akash is ready to be altered to match the purpose of your current life.

Dear ones, we've given the process before. Begin changing your fears by being proactive. Start practicing difficult things by walking into the very situations you don't want to walk into. Actively begin to steer into situations that you would never go to before. If you're shy, start talking to people without being asked. *"How are you?"* Pretty soon you realize it's easier than you thought, because you are changing the very engrams of your personality. Pretty soon you stop steering away from things you did before, because your innate body intelligence starts to cooperate with you. It shares your desire to erase the fears that are subconscious. You will have recalibrated them by *rewriting* them to match the new Human's energy. You're not going to cover up these "faults" with a program or a process.

Instead, they're going to go away because you are rewriting the information that used to be there with new information that you're actively creating.

EGO: The ego will never be a problem. You will be proud of yourself in a way that is appropriate and you never have to tell anybody how proud you are. You won't feel that you have to be validated. Spirit knows you! Spirit knows all about you. Isn't that good enough? The love of God carries you from place to place and says, *"We honor you. We love you."* That should be good enough! You never have to tell anybody anything about what you've done unless they ask. There's no desire to verbally spill it out and you won't want to. Never again will you open the conversation with, "Here's who I am, and here's what I did and here's what I've done." Even under the guise of self-help, "Here's how I helped myself", won't occur to you either, because you will be complete without this habit.

ANGER: Now this doesn't fit everyone in the room, but it fits some of you. Some of these things are hard to hear. Anger is an issue created by the energy of the past. You get angry because something *triggers* the anger. The trigger is *information*. You're programmed! You are programmed by your own chemistry to respond to things you don't even remember. Sometimes it's in the current life and sometimes not. It doesn't matter what it was created from, you're programmed and you know it because it makes you angry. You actually respond emotionally and your very chemistry starts to change. You have to admit, that's pretty profound!

How would you like to remove the anger trigger? If you rewrite the basic information that created the trigger, you'll never be angry. Oh, you could be disappointed, but not angry. Do you know how one can tell the difference? The Human will never have *rage chemistry*. That's chemistry in your body that makes your heart beat faster, raises your blood pressure , and literally blocks logic and common sense. All those things are basic survival "fight or flight" instincts and they belong in another time. There'll be no anger trigger when the information that causes it is gone. Anger will be something that is not one of the attributes of your life, and you'll start realizing it over a period of time. Disappointment? Yes. Sorrow, empathy and compassion? Yes. But not anger.

We have asked this before: Can you reach the point where a Human Being can point at you, call you names, and accuse you of things that are not accurate – and you can look them in the eye and the only thing that you will feel is empathy for them? No anger. No trigger. Is this really possible? Yes.

REACTION: Imagine no instant reactions to emotional triggers – no automatic defense. Can you reach a point where the things that you would normally react to don't affect you anymore? They carry no control over you at all. Reaction is an automatic response to a program within the attributes of your personality that seems to be beyond your ability to stop. You automatically defend; you automatically speak when you hear something that you don't like. What if you could totally rewrite that engram?

Oh, you may not agree with something. But why do you have to respond? Why do you have to defend anything at all? Dear one, when this situation happens, it's another person's idea of you. So it's their issue, not yours. What is there to defend? When God loves you to the degree that I have told you, and sees you as a divine Human Being walking this planet perfectly in lesson day by day, isn't that good enough for you? If a person accuses you wrongly, then be disappointed or empathetic for them. Be compassionate. Can you do that? You don't have to react. Their opinion does not change who you are.

JUDGMENT: What kind of judgment would you put upon those who would falsely accuse you? What do you think about those who are in ignorance or perhaps uninformed and who then go and do certain kinds of things that hurt you and perhaps others? What is your judgment of those who don't believe what you believe? How do you see them? This is one of the biggest issues, dear ones, believe it or not.

How does God see those of whom I speak? How does a master see them? Millions of Human Beings believe certain spiritual things that you don't necessarily ascribe to. How do you see them? In their zeal they tell you God will punish you if you don't do what they are doing exactly as they are doing it. So what do you see when you come into contact with them?

I'll tell you what the masters see, and let this be your test. The masters will say, *"Blessed is the Human Being who finds God anywhere in any way, for that is appropriate for their path. Do not judge the one who does not find God the way you have found God, old soul. For whatever they find is good enough for their path for now. Celebrate the fact that they even want to find the Creator inside in the way they do. If they want to climb steps and crawl and cry to have their spirit soothed, it is their way. If they want to assign creative source to a prophet, it is still honored. For they are looking for the same thing that you've looked for and all humanity is still looking for. Each Human has his own path in his own time. Look at all with honor and compassion, understanding and joy. That's how God sees them, old soul. It's time you understood this and did the same."*

We're getting down to the basics, are we not? Every single one of the five is a basic linear survival attribute and they all belong to a distant older Human Being who was you in many past lives. You may start rewriting these things even today. These are the attributes we want you to work on, for when you have accomplished even a partial rewrite of any of them, it's almost like a door opens and the things that you've asked for will begin to synchronistically manifest.

I wouldn't tell you these things if they were not accurate. This is the Human spiritual system at its best. Practice that which is mastery with the examples you've been given over history from the masters. Start to change who you are in order to move into who you will be. This is what is going to change the earth. This is the task of the old soul today. And so it is.

I am Kryon, in love with humanity.

The Wisdom of the Ages:

There is an alignment of the planet's wobble based upon the 26,000-year cycle of Earth. It has the potential opportunity for the movement and the creation of energy that you see today. The closer you get to this, the more the potentials grow. So even as recently as 600 years ago, it looked to the indigenous as though these predictions were a fact and not just a potential.

They started including the information in their calendars and you could see it in the glyphs on the walls of their pyramids. Ask an indigenous elder: "What's happening now? Is it what you expected?" The answer is, yes, right on schedule. But isn't it interesting that we have to tell you about this and it's not in your newspapers? You're not seeing it in your television either – not the truth. You're only getting pieces and parts of it.

The results of this shift are multifaceted. If you want to look at the grand result, it's going to eventually push humanity into a new reality, your future. But for now, there are seeds of compassionate action to plant, and the patience to let them grow.

Kryon

The Recalibration of the Crystalline Grid

This is the last *Recalibration of...* channelling and the last one given in 2012. As you have been reading so far, especially in Chapter Eight, the relationship betwen Gaia and the Human is profound. Here is still more information about how the shift in energy will impact everything from 2013 and beyond. Gaia changes, we change, and the future of the planet will be different.

Lee Carroll

Chapter Twelve
THE RECALIBRATION OF THE CRYSTALLINE GRID
Portland, Maine
August 2012

Kryon
Book 13

Chapter Twelve
The Recalibration of the Crystalline Grid
Live Kryon Channelling - August 2012

Greetings, dear ones, I am Kryon of Magnetic Service. My partner opens the door, and in the action of his spiritual intent, there is a meld that occurs. The conduit of communications on this planet called channelling is not that difficult to understand, for it is not what you would call a *possession* by another entity. Is God an entity? Can God possess you?

The channelling you are experiencing now is a meld between the Human Being's Higher-Self and the energy of what you call "the other side of the veil". But the *bias* of the Human Being wishes to assign a personality or an entity to whatever comes through, not understanding that this is not the way it works. Were the ones who wrote "the words of God" in scripture possessed?

I speak to you now through my partner's mind, using all of his experiences, his language and his intellect. It's all brought together right now so that as I project to him the thought groups I wish to communicate, it all gets linearized into his language and given to you. With his allowance of the process, another energy is created – a multi-dimensional one. This energy is one that is not audible, but you can feel it. In a true quantum state, there is no time. Therefore, anyone listening to this or reading it will receive that energy if they wish. If the reader wishes to give intent for the process, it will be just as fresh to them as it is to those of you who are here right now in person.

So we say it again: Long after this particular meeting is finished, there will be those still involved in this meeting, in the recordings or the transcriptions, and to them it will be *now*. So let me address those who follow, for we see the potentials of who they are and we see their eyes on the page. There is more here than meets the eye, dear ones, a lot more.

Why Are You Here?

I want to give you some information about why you are here. If we could give this in its simplistic form, it is about Gaia – the energy of Earth. It's also about all of you – those who have come from the creative source, the source that you call God, and those who come to this planet lifetime after lifetime in order to give the potential of peace on Earth and more. It's about your Higher-Self.

The potential of this planet is changing, and the change is right on schedule, for past planets who have gone through this same experience all reached the shift within 300,000 years of their *seeding*. The seeding on Earth represents the implementation of giving you the DNA that you received from the Plciadians, who were from the last planet that went through this process. This seeding is, therefore, your creation story, and represents that point in time when humanity itself was given the knowledge of dark and light. Planet after planet has been given this opportunity, one at a time. Some make it to the shift and some do not. You are currently the only one going through this and your current shift is still in its infancy. Because of your shift, you will eventually seed another planet. But that's a story for another time.

The last time we sat with you, we discussed some of the Human attributes that you have to get past in order to move cleanly into this shift. Sometime before that, we told you how young you are – that the Human race is very, very young while the earth is old. We told you the earth and the galaxy are all the same age; we told you that there is other Human-like life that has been in existence on other planets, even some in ascension status, thousands of years before the microbes started life on the planet Earth. Dear ones, it means you have a strong lineage in your DNA from those who begat those before you, and who also had the seed of God in them. Before the Pleiadians, they had those who seeded them, and those even before them. You are new, but your DNA imprint is very, very old. The time schedule of your shift is just about right for you, for it has been approximately 200,000 years since your seeding, and now you move into this energy shift.

What Is Next?

Now we discuss what is new and what is coming, which is different in an esoteric way. You've spent all of this time, Human Being, to get to the point where you realize that a high consciousness is a real possibility for the planet. Not all of you see this. Many Humans will only see the problems and the drama, but the old souls are aware, since they have been expecting it. It's a slow movement toward a planet without war. It's a slow agreement about new wisdom of the environment and looking for what may be next to accomplish it. The addition of new inventions is the key. You will have new discoveries that will enhance humanity's ability to have fresh water any time and very efficient energy so that even in the cold winters there will be no shortage of power and no issues with the potential of grid loss (there won't be a need for an electric grid). These are the things we told you that are coming. But let us talk of the esoterics (things based in energy, which are beyond current physics), for these are changing as well.

What is the goal of your experience on Earth? You are not here, dear one, to live lifetime after lifetime as an experiment. There is no experiment here. All this has a plan, a beautiful one. This is a *system,* and the system has this planet coming to the fruition of its potential, a time where Human nature itself will change. DNA will also change - not the chemistry you can measure, but the quantum energy that creates the Merkabah. This is the quantum part of the Human Being that metaphorically shines in a dark place. It is the *piece of God* that is in you, which starts to become active, and within the process the Human Being starts to think differently. It propagates itself through the rebirth of old souls to a place where they replace old consciousness, and it is slow.

In this time frame, you are approaching 21 December (2012), which is the mid-point of the precession of the equinoxes. All over the earth, time zone by time zone, it represents the mid-point of the 36-year alignment. The next 18 years are critical, starting in 2013, and this is where it gets esoteric. What is the goal? What is the mechanism of change? How does it work? We want to review this with you, for many will be reading this far beyond 2012.

The Crystalline Grid Explained

That which we call the Crystalline Grid is the mechanism of how humanity communicates with Gaia. It's not necessarily in real time, either, for it's cumulative. Let me explain: We have told you about a grid of the planet that is called crystalline. We have told you this is not something you can see, but it exists. It is a multi-dimensional, esoteric grid that covers the very dirt of the earth – all of it. It's under your feet now and it's wherever you walk. You might say it is a *shell of the planet that remembers Human energy*.

Crystalline attributes in geology are recognized scientifically as substances that can hold and store vibrational frequencies. So the metaphor of the Crystalline Grid is *a grid that holds memory and energy*. The energy that it holds best and that it was designed for is *everything Human*. The planet responds to you because of this grid. The consciousness of humanity is embedded into the grid through your actions every single day of your life, and everything you do has an energy of some kind.

For thousands of years, these energies that you have created as Humans have all been similar. Human nature didn't change much, so it was a repeat of the same things. You can see this clearly in your past, for history repeats itself : war repeats itself, government repeats itself, greed repeats itself, and this is where the shift begins. You're starting to see the subtle changes in your daily lives: your children are changing, governments are changing, and regular Human Beings are awakening to the shift that is before them that will change the very essence of how they live.

As we channel this, the governments that are currently failing have been here for a very long time. Their leaders are in total and complete denial, holding out to the very end, even to face death. They can't believe it's happening, for things have been the same for decades, and they feel they will be again. The ones before them and the ones even before them all had the same kind of control. It's about the disbelief and denial that Human nature is changing. There was a stability in the old energy, and that is now changing.

Everything that has happened etches itself onto the Crystalline Grid. For those of you who sense energy, let me ask you: When you stand in a battlefield that is only a few hundred years old, what do you feel? For those of you who sense this energy, you feel the emotion, don't you? Perhaps you feel the desperate sorrow or perhaps the release of death. Much goes on with Humans during a battle and the Crystalline Grid at your feet on this battlefield knows it all. It stored it!

The Changing Crystalline Grid

Up until now, the things that got recorded were always those things with the most dramatic emotion. If there was an emotional event on the planet, those who sense these things can go and stand where it happened and they will feel it. Quite often, it's the attribute of mass death and drama. These are also the things that Human nature remembers first and they are the most indelible – death and drama.

However, the attitudes on the planet are starting to change and the very attributes of what is important to Humans is starting to change. Perhaps even Human nature is starting to change. The planet is starting to shift, and the idea that you are headed for a swift end is diminishing. This old attitude is a result of hundreds of years of prophecy that represented a very old idea that these times would bring an end, not a beginning.

There will still be those, including some old souls and Lightworkers, who will stand and say, *"This and that cannot change because..."* and then they will give a list of doom attributes, which is a list of all the things that you've experienced in the old energy that are issues and problems that had no solution. The assumption is that they can't be fixed or changed and tomorrow will be worse than today.

Why do I tell you this? If you have a more enlightened popu-lation, there will be more wisdom. You will receive solutions to the unsolvable. You don't know what you don't know. If you live with black and white sight, and all of a sudden the children start arriv-ing with the ability to see in color, how do you think your actions are going to look to them? They will see things you never did. You will see these children as odd and strange, since they are talking about hues and colors and you are talking shades of black and white. That's what is happening. The very Earth will start to change how it works because *you are changing you.* This Crystalline Grid of yours has piled up all of these events of humanity and recorded them. This is the energy of the planet and it has been driven by feelings, emotions, death, love, joy and compassion. But within these, drama has been the king of energy for all these years.

Now I'm going to give you the attributes of how this is all changing. As you change yourselves, Gaia responds and starts to also become more multi-dimensional as it is echoing your shift. the Crystalline Grid is going to change the manner in which it remembers things.

The Biggest Change – The Way The Grid Remembers

The primary change: the Crystalline Grid is no longer going to remember in a linear way. Here is what that means. When energy adds to itself as you pile things up, it seems to pile in layers. The things on the bottom were first and the things on the top were last, and whatever this all adds up to is a linear, unchangeable total. There is an assumption that those layers are forever and you can't go in and change them. But what if you changed the *importance* of certain energies within the existing layers? What if all the drama that happened in the past got reduced in importance? Imagine the grid responding to this, and all the horror and drama in the past got reduced in energy within all the historic layers. Do you understand that this is impossible if time is linear? Linear time demands that it is static and unchangeable. What happened in the past is what happened – period. But quantum time is in a circle, so if the "rules" change, then as one thing in the layer changes, the energy of the whole circle changes.

If a quantum change were possible for the grid, then did you just change your past? The answer is no. The past is linear for you, but you can change your perception of how it gets remembered, and this is partially what the Crystalline Grid is doing – recalibrating itself for past, present and future. This, in itself, will change the planet.

Suddenly, the Crystalline Grid starts to clean itself of the old total (change the importance of the remembered layers) because now it is responding to light and dark differently. Up to now, it was driven mostly by things that were dark. That's Human nature. We have told you that less than one half of one percent of this planet has to awaken in order to have the entire planet change. Does that sound linear? No. But it's the same principle. Light is starting to trump darkness, and you are the ones who have this ability to impact the Crystalline Grid in a greater fashion than it has ever been impacted before. The old energy of the past, no matter how dark, will not have the effect it did before.

The Reaction of the Old Energy to a New Grid

The old energy on this planet creates a pattern and Humans have gotten used to certain things, including the way the Crystalline Grid works. Old energy counts on the Crystalline Grid remembering things that are more dramatic than things that are not. That means negative things have more energy than positive things. That's what is changing, and the old balance of dark and light will react. You see, there is a *consciousness* of the dark and light balance that is perceived within the Human. There is an old balance of dark and light that has been here for centuries, but when it starts to shift, Humans don't know how to react.

This is all metaphoric, describing the energies on this planet. But I will tell you that against all common sense, there will be those who take the old energy to their grave because they just can't help it. It's all they know. There will be those who will go yelling and screaming, not believing that what is around them is shifting and turning so greatly. You'll see it in government, you'll see it in politics, you'll see it in banking, you'll see it in insurance, and you'll see it in your drug companies. They are all counting on the old way things work.

The Crystalline Grid is starting to awaken and be responsive to light and compassion instead of drama. If a battle occurs on the planet, the grid won't "see it" the way it did before. Gaia herself won't record the drama of it, and won't respond as she did before. Do you know what happens when a war doesn't get any attention? Pretty soon there's no reason for it, and that's what we're saying. Only the things that make a difference to light on the planet will go into the Crystalline Grid and be measured differently. It will not measure darkness and drama the way it did before, and it will not see the emotion of hatred and terror the same way. The things that had the most impact on Human nature in the past that you now remember more than anything else – death, sorrow, murder – will not matter nearly as much. Oh, it will still be there, but it's not something you're going to want to hear about, dear one. Stand by for that.

There's going to be a day when you're going to go to your news and you're going to expect the *good news channel*. When the old style reporting tells you something awful has happened and they "churn it", it will hurt your heart, and you're going to turn it off! You will turn it off because it doesn't suit the magnificence of the God inside you! Do you understand what I'm saying? When enough of you turn it off, those who produce the news will realize it and start to understand that Human nature is changing. Then they will change.

The Result

Human nature itself will shift, and drama will not hold the key that drives the earth's grid anymore. That's the new news. This represents a difference, a recalibration in the way that you will communicate with the planet – a total and complete difference. That's what we want to tell you.

What are you going to make of this? What are you going to do next? Let me show you the profundity of this. There are those in this room with puzzles they don't know what to do with, and they are waiting for synchronicity and intuitive answers. In the process of the way you work with Spirit, dear ones, you become self-balancing. This means that no matter how unbalanced you become in 3D, there is a trigger that will create a self-balance energetically, and to which you will return automatically. You self-balance; that's what a mature, old soul does.

When you start to solve the problems that you came in with today, whether it's health or relationships or life's purpose, the solutions create light. This is a metaphor, dear ones, and the only way we can give you a visualization of what is happening. The solution to your problems, using the creator source within, creates another energy, which is light. Solution and balance create light, and this light is immediately seen by the Crystalline Grid. It sees it as fast as it saw drama before. Light goes into the grid and it changes the planet incrementally in a way it never did before.

So as you leave this place, making decisions that are going to enhance your life, you are creating light and generating compassion that the planet knows about and records. That's what you're here for. That's your goal, no matter what you thought you were supposed to be here for. Everything you do is about the creation of peace inside.

We've said it before. Sometimes we give Humans things to do to keep them busy! And you think you are working toward your goal? Your goal is to *exist and love God.* That's your goal, and in the process you have marriages and children and careers. There is sorrow and there is death during life. In the process, there are books that are written and friends who come and go. In the process, you self-balance and Gaia sees the light of your solutions through all of this.

When you are born, your spiritual instincts are driven by your Akashic inheritance [instinctual remembrance of what you have learned]. You know God is inside; You know that help is there; You know intuitively of your seed biology and the love of those who seeded you. All of those things are inbred in you, and it creates a Human Being who can do what no other Human Being can do at this point in time – change this planet!

It's going to take a long time to steer this change to a full reality for Earth. But now you've created the ladder where there was none before. You have started to build the bridge where none existed before. Do not fear what comes next, for there are those energies that wish to pull you back. These energies are blind and have no idea of the amount of light behind you that will push you forward. They are blind to the light. They'll scream and yell and go into their own demise in total denial, but you're an old soul and you've seen that before. Perhaps this sounds cryptic to you? For now it needs to remain so.

So, dear ones, *all is well*. Can you look at your life now and say that? All is well. Can you believe that there is purpose behind your life? Young person or senior, it makes no difference, because you will swap positions soon. It's what you do. And you're not going to miss the ending of this earth saga, I'll tell you that. All of you are coming back to participate in this renewing planet. This is what we see, dear family, because we've seen it before. This is a routine that you have felt many times but never on this planet called Earth. Now it's time.

That's the way it is today.

And so it is.

The Elusive Akash

I wanted to include at least a couple of channellings in the energy of 2013, and this is a good one. It's packed with information about how the "intelligent body" (innate) works with the brain. Why can't we more completely sense who we used to be? Were we really involved in past lives? There are some answers here.

Lee Carroll

Chapter Thirteen
THE ELUSIVE AKASH
Minneapolis, Minnesota
August 2013
Kryon
Book 13

Chapter Thirteen
The Elusive Akash
Live Kryon Channelling - August 2013

Greetings, dear ones, I am Kryon of Magnetic Service. My partner steps away from his consciousness in a move that has been practiced for years. This is not an easy Human attribute, for yet again the Human wants to be in complete and total control over those things that are most pertinent to their survival. One of these would be their consciousness, so the channelling that you see with him is a bit different from that of the past. We have said this before, that there is no *takeover* of the Human Being during this process. There is instead a meld, a partnership, and that is what you see. So as my partner steps aside, he is looking and watching everything that is taking place. He is even able to write it down later if need be. This is because we have a Human Being who is able to work with that sacred part of himself that is new and different. It's a *participation* instead of a takeover.

What you see in this new way gives the ability for humanity to participate intellectually and emotionally as the messages are given. This enhances the messages, for the Human who is in this channelled state is a translator. He is a translator using his language and moving through a system that is located in the portal of the pineal gland. The system is a multi-dimensional communication through a source that is in three dimensions [the pineal gland]. All of this is to say that what comes next, like so many other channels that we have given, is a combination of new information combined with things that we have stated before, but that have been spread over many channels. So now we coalesce these things into one message in order to bring forward a new concept.

The Human Akash

We want to speak more about the Human Being's Akash. Now, you will notice that we seldom use the word Akashic Record. This is because the very semantics of the word *record* give you a linear feeling of some kind of list, and we don't want you to think that way. Not only that, the Human Akash contains far more than a record of lifetimes. So this is where we are going to start today. We will go slowly so that any new concepts given will be explained correctly and well, so that you might understand them in their completeness.

What do you think about when we say Akash? We have named this channel *The Elusive Akash*, so we have already stated the attribute we are going to talk about. The Akash of the Human Being is a history of everything the Human Being has experienced on planet Earth. Now, there are more Akashic attributes inside you that go beyond humanism, but they are very well hidden and not the subject of tonight's message. So you might say that most of what you have that we define as the Human Akash is your direct experience on Earth. This Akash is also well hidden and it is elusive, but it shows itself all the time in ways that you don't recognize. So we start here by describing how it can actually be inside you, yet you would not be aware of it at all.

The Akashic Puzzle

Most Human Beings have no concept that they deal with the Akash every day. Most Humans are *driven* by it, yet they never know it. So I want to set the stage by telling you right now that the Akash is not something that communicates with you in a traditional way. It's not what you would expect. Let's back up a moment and look at the overview. The Akash is a system, dear ones, and it is beautiful. I sit in front of you knowing who is in the room and knowing about your lives, all of them. I know the puzzles you carry around today. I sit here as an advisor who has never been Human, watching you work a Human puzzle, which is amazing to me.

You are what you might call *a soul group* who are all specialists in *biological being expression* [Kryon's description of a group who specializes in walking through multiple Human lifetimes]. The creative source, which is God, who has made the Universe, the galaxies and all that is, has an elite grouping of specialists, and it's you! You are part of *the soup that is God* who specializes in doing what you're doing. It's a difficult role, so only a few trillion are selected to do it. If you want to know what's at the core of your soul as a specialist, it's love and compassion. That's the core. It's not always seen that way, but it's there, and when you come into the earth, your mission is to give it away - to share it with the very energy of the planet. The Akash is a system that helps to drive Humans into situations of learning and solution.

The attribute of the *piece of God* that you are, stays on my side of the veil. You come into the planet as a biological being and who you really are is hidden from you as you try to make your way through a dark earth. Hidden from you is how you are trying to find the light that's inside of your own cellular structure. You've got the hard work. All the masters who walked this earth tried to show you this Human God part and told you it was there. But it must be discovered.

Kryon has been here a long time. I was here with you when we watched the grids being set when the earth was being formed. It was just like before, when we watched other planets in other places being formed, knowing that someday you'd be doing what you're doing now, over and over and over. Certain groups of you come in first, and then others of you come later. That's the system. In this system, there is a real attribute of structure that honors consciousness, free choice and the concepts that we're going to talk about right now. All this is to say that the Akash is not a mistake or a mystery or a system of chance. It's a design, and it's designed to help you.

The Akash is intrinsic. It's there at the beginning and it came with you in your biology during your "awareness creation". It is a part of you that can never go away, can never be erased, and you live with it every day. It is part of the system you're born with, but it can be enhanced, understood, and changed to create your evolutionary process.

The Elusive Akash

Now, here is what makes this Akash elusive, dear ones. This system, this beautiful system, wants to be in your pocket as a help through your life all the time. But it responds almost completely to the *Human free will* attribute on the planet. If Humans decide that the planet should go backwards into darkness, the Akash behaves differently. If Humans decide that humanity will increase in Human consciousness, the light will begin to take over, and the Akash responds differently. So now you see that it's dynamic, and not "set at birth". It changes as you change. So the first thing is that it's always moving.

It is so elusive! If I ask any of you, *"Tell me about your past lives,"* the chances are that even the most enlightened of you would say, *"I'm not really sure. I may or may not have been here or there. I cannot seem to pick a separate lifetime out of the soup that is my consciousness. I have some strange memories, but I'm not positive that I might or might not have been this or that."* You'd be correct! So, why is the Akash so elusive?

The reason is this - listen carefully, for this is new information. The Akash is not a brain function. It is not where the synapse of memory occurs, so when you are trying to answer the Akashic question above, you are searching for these things in a structure of consciousness that works with common memory and synaptic attributes of the Human brain. The Akash is not in your brain, so you won't get the memories you are looking for. Instead, the Akash is in your DNA. So, suddenly we have a situation where Akashic communication is very different. It's not linear, and it's not able to be remembered like your brain remembers anything. It won't give you facts. It's elusive! So how does it *get* to you?

DNA communicates with you and your consciousness in a different way than your brain does. We have described this in the past, and it is complex. But I'll say it anyway: Information carried in your DNA has to get to your brain eventually in order for you to cognize it [become aware and believe it]. It then arrives in your consciousness and works a certain way, which we will describe next. It does so with what we call *overlapping multi-dimensional fields.* This is not a mystery of science, for in your electronics you have this type of communication all the time. DNA doesn't *talk* to you in memory, synapse, structure or linearity. It talks to you in *emotional concepts.* The process of overlapping multi-dimensional fields has a name in electronics, and it's called inductance. It's also the way that the sun transmits information and even astrological attributes through its heliosphere, into the magnetic grid of the planet through overlapping multi-dimensional fields. So this is natural, it's happening all the time, and it's fractal [has many repeating parts]. But it all happens at the basic DNA level. You have a field around your DNA that interacts with your consciousness through something we have called the "smart body" or *innate.* Don't over complicate this. Just know that the Akash is elusive because it does not allow you to remember as you normally remember things. It's not traditional. It's part of DNA communication.

How Does the Akashic System Affect a Human?

Let us speak of how it works, what the energy of it is today, and where it is headed. The Akash has what we call *drivers.* Drivers communicate certain feelings about the Akash into your brain, and it allows you to sense something. It does not come as memory, as we said, and the Akashic system does not necessarily feature the communication of an individual past life. [That may come later with DNA awakening and processing]. Normal Akashic drivers do not broadcast to the brain who you were, where you were, or when you were. There are no names and no genders, even though you may think you know. What it does instead is to give you *experiential, emotional concepts.*

The Akashic drivers for humanity, at the moment, are the same ones that have existed for eons. The things that you will sense first from your Akash, that drive themselves into your consciousness, are survival instincts. They are about past experiences that created *fear, drama and unfinished business.* You know I'm right. What is it you sense, old soul? It's what you're afraid of. The Akash will deliver this to your consciousness, not as a remembrance of what happened, but as a *survival emotion* of what happened. These Akashic attributes are called drivers because they drive you into action, or in many cases, non-action. You feel something, and you won't *go there* or do something because of what you feel. Is it intuition or Akashic remembrance? The concepts you receive are at the DNA level and they radiate to your brain and drive you through this exposure to the emotional part of your thinking. Why are these things such low energy? Why fear and drama? Why unfinished business and, yes, let's call it what it is - guilt. Why? You are an old soul! Don't you deserve something better than this? We have given you the information before. The energy of what you have created on the planet drives Gaia's consciousness and the efficiency of your DNA and the future of humanity. It represents your free will up to this point, and that's changing.

The Recalibration of Personal Akash

Imagine an Akash that is realigning its drivers. What if instead of fear, drama and unfinished business, the Akash started to present something else to you? It will, dear ones, for this comes with new energy and the recalibration that is going on right now. It represents a change in Akash communication, because you are increasing your vibration. All of the cells in your body know what is going on in this new era. You might ask right now, *"Well, Kryon, does that mean that everyone's Akash knows?"* The answer is, yes! The difference is whether the brain will allow it to be felt or not. Now, here is where the pineal comes in.

The brain also has its drivers, and some are spiritual drivers. You call them *filters*. Others call them *filters of belief.* The brain allows things to be cognized [believed] or not, based upon past experience and commitment to "the way things work". You are creating a new consciousness, and part of that is the allowance of the Akash to talk to it. Those in this room who are listening to this message and others who are listening and reading later may start to understand that as they increase the light of their awareness, they let in truth. It starts to change the communication of the Akash. The pineal works better, the filters are clearer, and the Akashic drivers start to change.

Much of humanity has filters that will not allow new spiritual thought. They are committed to their own box of belief and, while the DNA may broadcast new information, they are not "tuned to the station". But humanity is enabled for the shift, even though they may not receive it yet. This is the beauty of the system of the old soul, for you have created a worldwide enablement that can be "seen" by each and every Human if they wish to see it. Free choice is like that.

Now, in a moment, we'll talk about one of the most powerful and common drivers and how it works. But first I want to tell you there are always exceptions to the rules, because these things I am telling you are not absolute for every single Human Being. There are always those who are different. The reason is because your life's path, what you came for and what you are doing on the planet in service to humanity is unique to you. It's not generic to every soul. So as I give this information, it's an overview, and that's all I give you. So let's talk about one of the profound exceptions to the common Akashic drivers, and this is where you're going to start realizing that what I'm saying is accurate, since you can actually see it.

The child prodigy is not driven by fear, drama or unfinished business. The child prodigy who plays the piano like a master when he is four is driven solely and completely by his *craft*. The painter who paints like a master when she is eight is being driven by her *craft*, and that's all! The prodigy could care less about survival as long as they have their craft. It's all-consuming, very linear, and all they can think about. This creates a puzzle in psychology where you will have a Human Being without the possibility of having any remembrance of a complex talent they never could have experienced in this life, yet it's there. The puzzle for psychologists is: How could this be when it is not part of the brain's remembrance? DNA is *pushing* it to the brain as fast as the brain will receive it. It's the craft of many lifetimes. *Where do your hands go? How do you hold the brush? What are the notes on the keyboard? Do you remember the music?*

These are special cases, dear ones, but you see it often enough for you to know that it doesn't fit with synapse and memory. That is the Akash at a multi-dimensional level, pushing something to the child that's conceptual - art, music, poetry and sculpture. It takes lifetimes to make a master artist, and they will be born over and over, continuing with the craft that they had before. All they want to do is keep going with it. That's very different from your process, and the possibilities of all the things that I've talked about are reduced to *one thing* for them, the one focus for them, and you get to see it in a child prodigy. By the way, this is why so many artists are dysfunctional, for this continues and they are oblivious to survival reality and others around them; they are only interested in themselves and their craft.

Karma

The thing that drives most of humanity is one of the drivers you have labeled *karma*. Now, karma is much more than just unfinished business. Karma is not punishment for past deeds, dear ones. That's an attribute of judgment, which is not of God. Karma is sensing past experience and having an emotional response so that you will either do it again or stay away from it. Karma is powerful and most Humans feel it, but have no idea they are receiving a specific driver from the DNA's Akash. Karma often doesn't even feature completion! Sometimes it's a policeman becoming a policeman, or military men becoming military men again, or mothers becoming mothers. It's a driver of remembrance of both positive and negative things. Sometimes it's just emotion. Sometimes it drives someone into a classic mindset that is problematic.

You want to know that classic? It's a classic issue that psychologists really have a hard time with. It's hard to describe, but you will know it exists when I describe it. Sometimes things that you sense from the DNA are not pleasant, but you *remember* them as *who you are* - and you can't live without them. That's karma. There are Human Beings who come into life and who are convinced they don't deserve to be here. If that is their consciousness, the DNA tries to cooperate with it. You knew that, right? Cellular structure takes its cues from Human thought. Lack of self-worth will manifest itself with problems that create, you guessed it, more lack of self-worth. It also creates drama, and some people just can't seem to get away from it.

The Human who is abused early in life has many choices. They probably created the puzzle to see if they can break the pattern (karma at its best). Sometimes, however, it just validates what they feel, that they shouldn't be here. So that Human will often get out of one abusive relationship and move into another and another!

Friends will look around and say, *"What's wrong with you? You keep making the same mistake!"* At the Akashic level, they are responding to the same instructions over and over. It's a victim comfort zone. Do you see this?

This is what the Akash does. It presents to you concepts of existence. It will make you afraid if you've been afraid before. If I told you, dear ones, that you had been killed because of your beliefs, you'd probably believe me. Most old souls have been. If I asked you how many times it happened or where it happened, you'd be guessing. See what I'm saying? The Akash deals in concepts, not factual memories. It also gives you concepts that are invitations to change.

Past Lives in the Akash

Some interesting concepts are transmitted through the Akash. Let's talk about past lives. Past lives carry the concepts into the Akash that are inherited [Akashic inheritance]. So, if you were a warrior and were killed in the battlefield, you may not like the smell of gun smoke. These things are passed to you in unusual ways. Some of you can stand in a battlefield and smell it! Some of you like it, since it's the smell of victory and release - more emotional concepts. But you know there's something there and, dear ones, that's a concept. It goes into your central sensory perception. That's the Akash at its best. You're not *remembering* as much as you are *feeling* something that exists to this day inside you.

The past life reader has to sort all this out. They have to linearize something that is not linear. It's elusive, you see. Past life readers can sense the quantum field around you created by the DNA [The Merkabah]. This is where a good reader can help pull out individual lives from that "soup of concepts" that you would never be able to do. This explains how a good reader can help you with blocks and past experiences that you can't seem to get yourself.

Now, the old soul has an added Akashic attribute. The old soul, the one who has been here by definition for thousands of years, and lifetime after lifetime has experienced just about everything there is to experience. So what do you think is in your Akash, old soul? I will tell you: It's the same as everyone else's - drama, fear and unfinished business, until now. The old soul has a storehouse of awakening lifetimes and that's the difference. In the new energy that is what the old soul is going to start remembering. So being an old soul up to this point didn't hold nearly as much *weight* in the Akashic way as it does now.

Things are recalibrating. This is a recalibration of the Akash as well. It's how you feel, what you do with it, and how it drives you to do things. The most interesting attribute within the old soul is that old souls feel they have things all figured out. Been there, done that. There's nothing new, and in that they have cognized and committed to a way of life, or what they think is a way of life, on planet Earth. It's so interesting, and often totally wrong.

The Atlantis Syndrome

I gave this scenario before and I want to give it again just to preview this to you. I know it's controversial to many of you. How many of you were on Atlantis? As the many hands go up, I say to you, *"Really? Which Atlantis were you on?"* You would then say, *"Well, I was unaware that there was more than one!"* There were far more than one, dear Human. Let me ask you, *"What happened there?"* Then you might say, *"We had this advanced society and we were terminated because we did something wrong. This stays in our Akash and we know it."*

There are some concepts that you bring into your Akash that are extremely Human. I'm going to call one of them, "God, Gaia, and Creative Source of the Universe with a Human brain". Humans apply their own intellectual process to everything that is God. The Greeks did it very well. They created their gods to be above

Humans, but their gods were totally dysfunctional! They had all kinds of problems, complete with jealousy, hatred, vindictiveness and even incest! Their gods didn't like each other very much, just like Human families. They toyed with the Humans below just to irritate other gods. There was judgment, anger and rage. That's the mythology of the Greeks. They created gods with Human attributes.

Well, of course, you're way above that today. Instead, you've got one God who is love. But then somehow there was a war in heaven, and a fallen angel and anger and judgment and grief. The fallen angel is after your soul, of course, and so on and so on. Mythology continues. Dear ones, your societies have simply done the same thing the Greeks did, only it's a little more modern. This all comes from the Akash, believe it or not. It's a conceptual belief that consciousness is the same all over the Universe and, of course, it's Human consciousness. You are really not aware of anything more intelligent than you are, so you don't have any other concept for God.

In addition, you have the beautiful entity Gaia getting angry and striking you with lightning or drying up the ground so you can't have crops for food. Do you see what I'm saying? How much energy goes into ceremony to help make Gaia content? Centuries of Humans did that. This comes, literally, from the old soul. The longer you've lived on the planet, the more you associate your consciousness of humanism with any other consciousness that you see in the Universe.

So why the Atlantis issue? Alright, I'll explain it yet again, Lemurian. You got off that large mountain of Hawaii when it started to sink. It was your home for thousands of years - the highest mountain on Earth. It started to recede or sink as the bubble of magma began to vent itself through several of the volcanoes and release the pressure that had pushed it up. You had no idea if the whole mountain was going to disappear or perhaps even explode!

So over many years, most of you took to the sea and escaped. When it stopped sinking, some stayed, and the peaks of the mountains became your current Hawaiian islands.

Do you know what Lemurians love to do and what is in their Akash to this day? Lemurians look for other islands to live on. It's in the concepts of what they have in their DNA, which tell them that this is the way to live. It's a *concept of being* and many Lemurians over history ended up on other islands because they felt like home. However, many islands are also volcanoes. Often, through the natural recourse of geology, volcanic activity and earthquakes would take place and the islands would go under. Did you know that was in your Akash, old soul?

So what do you think you did next, Lemurian, after another island sank? Most of you would escape - and look for another island! The next lifetime, you would look for still another island! It's interesting, but it's extremely Human, that when bad things happen, you blame something or someone somehow - usually yourself. That's the old soul's *lack of self-worth* that we have spoken of so often. So now you are guilty about it, and now you've got another consciousness going on that says the island did something to you. That's the negative Gaia Effect that supposedly Gaia is angry. The real Gaia Effect is actually a beautiful cooperation with Human consciousness! But your Akash, which is very elusive, will give you a totally different concept.

So the old soul remembers Atlantis incorrectly. Atlantis is simply a generic name for any island you lived on that destroyed itself while you were on it. Most islands were surrounded by water for good reason . As we said, many were volcanic. Sometimes they were in vulnerable places, easily covered by water through earthquake and flood. Sometimes it would be cyclical with the water cycle every 1500 to 2000 years. Count on a Lemurian to be there! Did you ever think of that? This is not to discount Atlantis itself, but to tell you that there were many of them and it sticks in your conceptual DNA as one big event.

Regarding advanced technology, let me tell you what you "remember" as advanced technology. It's not what you have today. It's *high-minded conscious thinking.* That's your high tech, because on an island you can get together like you did in Lemuria and raise the vibration of the land that you're on. It's not about machinery and blinking lights. It's about a consciousness that could change physics.

The New Akashic Drivers

Turn the page with me for a minute. I now want to tell you about the new drivers of the Akash. They are *compassionate action, love, and finishing business.* These drivers are going to be broadcast from the old soul DNA to old soul brains. This will start a process of helping them think out of the box of traditional thought. Old souls will start to see that they are not victims of life. They belong here! Self-worth will increase, for it will know that Humans deserve to be here. It's time!

This process will allow the Akash to speak to the brain and the innate body in higher concepts, those of compassion. Ask a surgeon about how Human Beings often keep themselves alive in a hospital for months just to see a grandchild graduate. Ask a doctor if he's ever seen mind over matter. A doctor who works closely with death and dying will have amazing stories about how Human Beings can get up from their death beds when some of them decide they are worthy of being here. What do you think of spontaneous remission? This is the Human changing course.

The Results of New Consciousness and a Changing Akash

The Akash speaks to you through concepts. The new energy carries different survival drivers for the old soul and concepts where there is no more karma will be delivered into your brain.. It has been voided, as we told you more than 20 years ago [Kryon Book One]. We told you to drop karma, for it is not needed anymore. Go forward with Akashic energy that you create yourself for your future instead of a concept from the past.

Some of you are mystified and feel odd, because without the driver of karma you feel empty. Well, let me tell you, it's time to understand what that feeling is. It means that you control your life! It means you're not a victim of the circumstances that push and pull you around. You've dropped the old energy driver of karma and so now it's time to create! That's conceptual, and Human Beings who don't get that message think there's something wrong. Some liked the other feeling and equated it to "being normal". It's a recalibration. No more karma.

Past lives will not have the influence that they used to and the things that you used to remember about the past are starting to recalibrate. Now you will begin to remember success, love, compassion, and results that come through high thinking. You are going to want these things again. Do you see where this is going? Imagine a Human Being who is driven only by positive things. Imagine a Human Being who is driven so completely by positive things that he/she will develop books and television shows and movies about positive things. Imagine how that might change what others see and feel. Imagine how the few can show something to the many, which might change the planet! Imagine the funding for these things being easy, because old souls with money will see it, too!

Dear ones, you are going to start remembering, not old mythology, but the *reality* of God. You are part of the puzzle, and you now carry the solution. You deserve to be here, and the more you awaken, the longer you are going to live. Consciousness awareness of a compassionate mind will extend your life. You will never see an angry God in your compassionate mindset. You will never see the mythology of a creator who has judgment. That never existed! It's a Human thought placed upon God. Gaia will become your partner on Earth, not a frightening force you have to give offerings to any more than you would a Human partner. You will fall in love with Gaia. Do you see the differences? This is the elusive Akash, which is recalibrating itself to become a lot less elusive. This pushes Human Beings into a whole new *consciousness of being.* Then you start realizing that the masters of the planet all had it.

In closing, we ask you yet again: Who is your favorite master? Who? Put yourself with him or her right now. How do you feel? Your answer will be, *"Relaxed, peaceful, safe, so good!"* So I ask you again, what did they have that would allow you to feel this way? The answer is what you are learning to have for yourself: it's peace where there is no 3D reason to have peace, calmness where there is no 3D reason for calmness, an awareness of beautiful, esoteric things that are out of the sight of those who only trust what their eyes can see. It's the love of God that becomes prominent in your life and completely voids the lies of victimization and fear. You are relaxed and treat others differently. The Akashic concepts of mastery are manifested in your daily life, and things that used to be a problem simply become parts of the challenge of Human living and not a survival issue felt at the core level or pushing your "buttons" of fear.

Some of you in this room and those reading needed to hear that last part and you know what I'm talking about. Isn't it time to get rid of that old process? Why are you letting these things drive you into frustration? It's making you older. You can let it go now. Say it out loud if you want to. Let your cells hear it! The catalyst to an enlightened planet is sitting in front of me. It's the old souls who will allow these things to take place in their lives and live longer because of it.

There are those in the audience who have come for a healing. Let it be. Let it start now. Allow yourselves to get up from where you are knowing that it has begun. I want to tell you something that you may not be aware of: Every cell in your body knows what I'm talking about. They are all listening and cheering, if you'll allow them to. You're in charge of it all.

The brain is the great *central station* of the transit of consciousness energy. You are in control of what you will and will not allow into it. It's time to allow a new Akash to speak to you of the glory and the majesty of the system that you helped create.

That is the message for the day. I am Kryon, in love with humanity - and for good reason.

And so it is.

Kryon

The Three Winds

This final channelling is a wonderful description of how Kryon sees us, and it helps to explain the circle of life. Spirit sees us as one family member, one soul, going in a circle of life experience, which we as humans linearized into our history. But the past is simply part of a current energy pattern to God, and it is constantly being "rewritten." Confusing? Yes! Karma and contracts are again discussed, and also (gulp!) the information that we all have Pleiadian DNA. Hey, I've been accused many times as being off-worldly. Well, I am! The fun part is... so is everyone!

Lee Carroll

Chapter Fourteen
THE THREE WINDS
Calgary, Alberta, Canada
February 2013

Kryon
Book 13

Chapter Fourteen
The Three Winds
Live Kryon Channelling - February 2013

Greetings, dear ones, I am Kryon of Magnetic Service. The time between when I last spoke to you and now doesn't even exist for me. It is difficult to explain to a linear Human Being what it is like not to have time. All things occur at once, so it's an odd thing to talk about, for in your minds your future is not known to you and your past cannot be revisited. So to you, your existence is always in the present. However, on my side we are in all three realities, but we call it the *now*. These concepts are only energies, but you assign a 3D time location to each of them.

For instance,

THE PAST: Past actions in 3D cannot be changed, but the memories of them can. Therefore, if you rewrite your reaction to something that happened in the past and it changes YOU in the present, then what have you done? You just visited the past and have rewritten it!

THE FUTURE: You say your future is not known to you, yet the potentials of what you might do are indeed known. As you change your mind today, in a certain way you are then changing the potentials of what you may do tomorrow. Therefore, rewriting the future is doable today. When you make an appointment to go somewhere tomorrow, does that make you a fortune teller when you arrive at the scheduled event? If you cancel the appointment at the last moment, did you change your future? *"Wait a minute, Kryon. These are things we have control over, so it's not the same as a future that is a mystery to us."* What if I told you that to us, there is no difference. "Appointments" are scheduled and unscheduled in a reality that you can't easily see in 3D, but they are still potentials you create for yourself. We see it all as one thing, and it helps us to give you the kind of channel we're going to give you in this transcription. We're going to call this channel *The Three Winds*.

Much of this information has been given in pieces and parts over many years, but now we are putting it together. You've heard some of the terminology and we have alluded to it before, and now we wish to lay it all out as a carpet that will contain many answers and perhaps some controversies. Some of these things may not agree with what you might have heard from others, and this is where your divine discernment comes into play, for your intuitive sense should now be used to see if these things I'm going to tell you make sense or not. You can start to use what I call *spiritual logic*.

The Human Soul

First of all, the Human Being and the Human Being's soul are seen as one item to us. It is never split up in our reality and is in many places at once. But for your understanding and for this lesson, we have the soul in only four places at once. The three winds are three of the four, and the other place your soul resides is *home*. That's where I am, dear ones, and we don't call it a *wind* because there is no wind when you're at home. There is no action for or against, and there is nothing pushing or pulling. It is so difficult, if not impossible, to describe something to you that is so close to you, yet so hidden. *Home* is not one of the winds, for it is where you always are.

A piece of God is in you, yet what it is like to be on my side of the veil will remain hidden as long as you are a Human. It has to, for the test of energy that you are working on as a Human must remain in a certain kind of reality and consciousness for you to exist on the planet and work the puzzle. But there's no *wind* when you're home. Home is the place you are when you are not in one of the winds. Home is your natural "God state".

How Humans "See" God

You're a piece of the *soup of God,* which is measured in innumerable parts, yet all is one. The very essence of *entanglement* [a physics term describing a quantum attribute where things are locked into one reality regardless of distance] is an attribute of God. When you are in touch with your Higher-Self, you are in touch with all the parts of you. Sometimes Humans think that they're getting messages from angels, and these angels are given messages from other angels, and so on and so forth. Humans see a hierarchy of authority in everything, since it exists in their own reality. But with God there's no such thing, for the wisdom of God is a singular wisdom which is always the same wisdom and is fully present all the time, everywhere. The truth is the truth, and because you have a piece of God in you, you become aware of an absolute truth as you awaken spiritually. This is why you can take an awakened Human Being from another part of the world that is foreign to you, speaking another language that is not yours, and find the same truth. The God inside you is the same as the one inside them.

So as we give this lesson, honor your intuition, that part of your mind that discerns using spiritual logic. Some of you may actually have a revelation of what we are speaking of as we discuss the Three Winds.

The Three Winds

Human Being, there is nothing more honored within the Human life scenario than the Three Winds. They represent one of the three states that Humans are always in. Two of them are brief and one of them is long. There is the Wind of Birth, the Wind of Existence, and the Wind of Transition. In your words, you would say birth, life and death. We don't use those words since they are biased to a 3D reality, which often is your only view of the truth.

The Wind of Birth

In each "wind", we're going to start by dismissing the fallacies and giving you the truth. So let us discuss as much as we are able and start with the energy at the Wind of Birth. The Wind of Birth is different from the actual physical event that you call *birth*. For us, the Wind of Birth is you right before you enter (taking your first breath). Imagine yourself as a piece of the whole, a part of the love element of the Universe, and a part of the wisdom of God. You're ready to go back to your planet, but you do not have the mind of a Human. What is involved? What energies spin around it that get you to this place? Who is able to be in the Wind of Birth and is there a system?

These things are difficult to describe, for they are not linear. Understand that you are aware of only linear things, since that is your reality. Your 3D reality as you sit there reading is only aware of one solitary life on Earth. But in this quantum Wind of Birth, we are *seeing* you standing at the precipice of another reality, returning to the planet after many lifetimes [speaking to old souls now]. So as you stand there, you are about to reconnect as a Human Being into the planet's energy in a certain way. The "wind" of the 3D reality you are about to step into blows against you with great force. You seem to "lean into it" as we make our final love words to you. You are about to disconnect from the reality of Spirit, willingly give away your memory of all that is, and return to Earth yet again. What a beautiful time!

What are the attributes or "rules" of this as you connect again to humanity? First, let me tell you what they're not, for so much of this is misunderstood. The first thing you should know is that the Human Being is absolutely unique. On this planet of the coming and going of sacred souls, Humans all have a divine part that we call the Higher-Self. All 3D Human DNA structure and the potentials within are identical. The only things that differentiate one from the other are within the quantum DNA portions – the energy of the Akashic Record.

The Power of the Akash

The Akashic Record holds within it the potential for enormous energy, depending upon what the Human has done in past lives. If the Human has awakened to spiritual potential before, then there is more energy than if they had not. Therefore, the potential creation of an enlightened old soul is literally available at the Wind of Birth, for it's about prior knowledge and experience and what you've done before on the planet. It's about who you were, what you accomplished, if you ever awakened to the workings of the *light puzzle* before or not, if you are returning or if it's the first time.

So the Akashic Record is not just a record of how many times you've been here, but rather how much spiritual knowledge and life experience you have awakened to through all your planetary experience. The Akash is a sacred library that you pick up and hold through each lifetime and then into the next. You add to it every time you come and go on the planet, and it helps to develop and alter what your next life may be about. Remember the axiom we have given in the past: *You will never have to return to a less-aware state.* Once you open the metaphor of the "spiritual Akashic jar", all spiritual learning and all accomplished learning are available from all lifetimes.

Your Biology Is Not All from the Earth

The Human Being's soul is a piece of God and is unique on the planet. However, biologically, the Human is not *an animal of Earth.* In fact, your unique Human chemistry proves it, since you have "fused DNA" that creates the 23 chromosome separation from the rest of Earth biology. You did NOT evolve from Earth!

The Human species as you see it today is not the Human species of 200,000 years ago. So the first realization for you is that your entire corporeal existence is not as "an animal of your planet", despite what biologists will tell you. There was help along the way with an "awakening to light and dark" within your DNA. Even the most basic of religions tell you about this event as the divine "creation story" common to all humanity. The Human you are today is unique in the Universe and has amazing creative powers, just as the masters of the earth all told you.

The Animal System

Animals have their own kinds of energies, and some of them even have their own kinds of animal soul-groups. Animals are on the planet for several reasons, and we've told you all this before. However, all of them are on the planet as part of the balance of Gaia, and many as *friends to Humans*. They hold the energy of life for Earth, and sometimes they are here to love.

Certain kinds of animals have animal souls and incarnate within their own groups, but they are always in service to humanity. Their own soul groups come back as animals – only animals. They do not cross the soul barrier into a Higher-Self being. Animals do not *graduate* into Human Beings, although it is very easy for Humans to think they do, because this is the way Human thought has always worked for you. In your opinion, you graduate into higher levels and then you become better. Therefore, those who would look at the scheme of life would probably say, *"A soul starts as an animal and then works its way up to become Human."* However, this is not the case and never was, dear one. A Human Being has a beautiful Higher-Self, which is the core soul of God energy; animals do not have this.

The Human Spiritual System

The puzzle during your life is about how much of this truth of being part of the Creator you can accept. How far can you open the quantum door to see this truth when you are alive? This single attribute determines how enlightened you become during life. Listen: It's not how much knowledge and experience are in your Akash, but how much you allow yourself to believe it. There are many old souls on this planet who have an amazing amount of spiritual learning, yet they don't want to touch that "spiritual jar" within them at this point in their lives. This is the free choice of the Human Being that we speak about.

There is immense planning that puts you at the Wind of Birth. What did you accomplish during our recent lives, if anything? Who were you and what did you do? What energies did you start that were not complete that you wish to continue? What soul group were you in? Who were your parents? Are you in certain soul agreements to become their grandchildren? That is more common than you think! There are so many things that go into the planning of the "entry energy" of your life, and each life potential is different and unique. The planning is done by you when you have "the mind of God" on my side of the veil.

Humans don't like the fact that there is no generic spiritual instruction manual that states, *"Here is what happens and here is what to do."* Listen, dear ones, humanity is honored way above that! Are all your children the same? Do books on how to raise children always work for your child? The answer is no, because each soul is totally unique. But Humans still wish to have a list of things to do and not to do, as though each soul somehow came out of a spiritual machine that made them all the same. No. Instead, Spirit honors each soul with unique choice and a tremendous variety of energy selections.

The Great Artists

There are certain attributes that Humans receive on the planet, and we'll call them creative attributes. These are almost quantum attributes that may take several lifetimes to complete. What often happens to these *creatives* is that they go through a series of lifetimes *as though it were one* in order to have completion of their creative cycle. Famous artists will come back, and the first thing they want to do is pick up a brush and continue what they did before. Famous composers, famous poets and sculptors will come back and simply keep going! It's so obvious, yet you deny this in your scientific way.

So the creatives are different from the others, and their puzzle is to bring the greatest treasures of art to the planet through a unified series of lives, yet personally they try to sort out the puzzle of "what they carry inside is valuable, but nobody knows it". If you've noticed, most of the great artists who have ever lived and who are here today carry a burden that is easily identified as "lack of self-worth". Do you see the set-up? It's ripe for personal discovery, isn't it? So can you see the Human standing in the Wind of Birth, ready to continue what they only began last time? With the "mind of God", there is a smile on their face as they *hear* the music that they will compose, for it's with them when they arrive.

As you stand at the Wind of Birth, you are completely and totally a unique creature with incomplete energies. It takes more than one short earthly life to create Human attributes that grow into maturity. Even non-creatives (most of you) have a lineage of starting something that never got fully completed. Sometimes it's in relationships. Sometimes it's learning or teachings. Old souls are good at this coming and going and often pick up where they left off as they slowly change the planet by their very presence upon it. The old soul is, " *Sowing the seeds of light on the carpet of linear time, not even knowing that they will also be harvesting those exact mature plants of wisdom as they return in a subsequent life.* "

Therefore, dear one, you don't *arrive* with a blank slate, but you know that, don't you? The old soul feels it. The only ones who arrive with a completely blank slate are the newbies [first timers] and we'll talk about that in the next *wind*. But this is a room of old souls who are hearing and reading this right now. Each of you is here with a spiritual jar that is filled with the experience of living on Earth, and sometimes even the attribute of "awakening to your own mastery".

Akashic Readers

There are those who can read your Akash. But unlike a linear file cabinet, they can't read the lifetime in some linear way. Instead, they'll see the energetic lives that stick out, the ones that have a profundity about them for you. These are the lives where you accomplished things, or perhaps even worse, you didn't. There are the lives where dramatic things happened such as early death, loss of children, or battlefield experiences. It's all based on energy and potentials. You'll hear that again, since it's important.

You are standing at the Wind of Birth and you're about to come back to the planet. Laid upon you are all the potentials and possibilities based on your past experience and the imprint of "who you are." You're coming back as part of the spiritual family of Earth, which is what your soul group does. Where will you be? What gender? The most difficult thing for me to describe to you is that the planning is not linear and it is not something that you would see on a logical financial spreadsheet. It's energy-based and very often influenced by others. It's, therefore, also family-based.

If you have awakened to spiritual truth in a past life, there is strong potential it will greatly change the next life. So an old soul will go to another place that perhaps a young soul would not go. All of this is in the planning before the Wind of Birth, and you're ready for it. You really are. Listen: No Human soul comes to the planet unwillingly or as punishment. Perhaps you should memorize that statement!

The Biggest Change...

Old soul, right before you come back to the planet, the energy is completely different at the Wind of Birth because of what has happened in the last 20 years. In this new energy after 2013, the old soul who is coming back with that *spiritual library* filled with spiritual purpose is *comfortable* with this process. S/He intuitively remembers very fully what he has been through. Did you hear that? This is different than the last time! This is a result of everything that has happened in these last years. You have changed the rules!

The old soul is not going to be subject to some of the energies that push and pull a younger soul. The old soul has made up his or her mind as part of the planning about what they are going to do that they could not do before within an older energy. This is only possible since they can now plan on having the spiritual jar intuitively open early in the new life. The old soul may even know this now and plan for it before the end of his/her current life, intuitively knowing about the next life during the current life. This is the difference, dear ones. It's the beginning of "intuitive spiritual logic".

We've told you in previous channels about some of the interesting differences between new Humans and ones like you, who have been born into an older energy. We've told you that the quantum DNA alterations that you have created by living many lifetimes of awakening to enlightenment and knowledge will now allow you to be a very different child in your next life. You will be a child who *remembers* how to read instead of one who is *taught* how to read; a child who can walk earlier and talk earlier, because s/he *remembers* how. This is because the bridge in the DNA is starting to be complete between *what was* and *what is*. What this means is that the DNA is starting to quantumly change into its original state of being, which is far more efficient. You will see it first in the children and, dear ones, don't expect to see it in a microscope. Instead, you will have to eventually ask a sociologist to prove any of this, for it will be seen first as a change in Human behavior.

Therefore, old souls will come in as Humans who will not need to start over and be taught everything from scratch, but instead will arrive with a *full load* of intuitive past-life experience. As their brains develop, they may even remember who they are [old souls who have been here before]. This is the promise of the new energy, especially after 2013. You're going to see changes in some of your children and grandchildren as they arrive and grow up. The stigma of a planet that is going to be destroyed by war or by God will not be among the energies of the new ones. The promise of a planet going into new, uncharted areas of quantum discovery will be upon them. They'll need a whole new set of tools.

Who Has Gone Through This?

Oh, you have all participated in this *wind*. Everyone in the room has participated in this. You stood there knowing what the life lessons were and the potentials of what was next due to what happened in previous lives. These were not mistakes, dear ones. These were the results of potentials and plans you made for your own soul.

There is no *newbie* here in this room [to be explained]. Not all of you listening and reading, however, are old souls in the classic sense – souls who have been here hundreds of times. But you have been here before, so this counts as one who has walked through the process many times. It's what makes you interested in this material. Did you think of that? There is great variety in the understanding of this knowledge among you. It is absorbed very differently between you. Some will sleep through it and others will be spiritually awakened by it [Kryon smile]. It depends on where you are on the path you planned. Again, each path is unique.

The Wind of Existence

We arrive now at the Wind of Existence. This is what you call *life*. Let us give you the attributes. First, no matter what you have been told by spiritual *authority*, you are not here as punishment. You're not here to be tested. Sometimes we call your life a *test*, but it's a test of *energy*, not of you! Gaia then measures the energy of the planet and passes the results to the very fabric of time and existence – to the Great Central Sun. It's the measurement of the vibration of the earth via the Crystalline Grid, which plays a part in a much larger scenario that we have not discussed much.

Therefore, the *test* is whether Humans can change that earth measurement by their consciousness. That's the test. Again, Humans are not here to be tested, but rather you're here as family. The bridge between the Wind of Birth and the Wind of Existence is not subtle. It's where you remove everything you know about the truth and come in with it blocked out. When you step into that Wind of Birth, you're no longer aware that you are a piece of the Universe. There is no longer the connection to the consciousness of God itself. You don't *remember* where you came from or what you've been through.

The newer energy now has you awaken to intuitive *potentials of remembering* these truths. They are in your Akash, but available only through intent. As we have indicated, some old souls don't necessarily awaken at all! Sometimes an old soul who has had a very difficult and profound previous lifetime will soar through this current life as a *vacation* from spiritual things and never claim they are interested. But, dear ones, you know who they are when you meet them and you can see it in their eyes. Some of you have even married them! They may not be here at a meeting like this either, but it's the energy of this very thing that originally attracted you.

The Old Soul's Purpose

Dear ones, you have to understand the uniqueness of life. It's why we say there are no rules that state that you somehow must awaken to help the planet or that you have to send light while you are here. There simply are no *have tos* because the system is complex with variety. This time around, some are simply here to hold the energy of who they are and where they are. The next time around they will do the work, but for now they just hold a place. Some of you have had these very attributes and it's necessary and needed on the planet. Like a spiritual relay race, some carry the baton swiftly and some sit and watch, but *all* are part of the event.

Some old souls are simply holding the energy, unaware of any metaphysical journey at all. So this would be like *old soul recalibration or rejuvenation.* However, some of you might say, *"I'm not certain I like that. It seems like a waste of an old soul's life – of 80 years or more!"* Dear ones, is it a waste of three weeks when you go on vacation? No. You often come back rested and ready to work! It's complex and you look at things in the light of "a lifetime". But for us, it's simply a passing day. It's all about timing. So don't make up your mind about what is working and what is not, based on your "lifetime clock".

Old souls will have the greatest impact on the planet in the new energy. The ones who have been here the most often will know better what to do than ever before about the conditions they find when they arrive.

The Wind of Existence Categories: New and Learning

NEW: The newbies are always arriving. They have to, because the planet has a geometric expansion [population growth] rate. So logically, do you understand that there are new souls arriving all the time? It's obvious. You can recognize a newbie in a minute when you start talking to them. You say A and they hear B. You'll ask them to go left and they'll walk right. They'll have no idea about anything, how anything works between Humans. They don't really understand if a thing is good or bad. Appropriateness of behavior is a mystery – and it often shows.

They don't know how life works in general. You will slap your head in amazement because you can't believe anybody could be that way! They're new. They don't know about Human nature. They're the ones who can be easily tricked by another Human Being. Again, you will slap your head and think, *"Did they just arrive?"* Yes, they did.

They are naïve to the max in all directions and you've seen them. Each of them will have to come back a number of times before they start to understand the whole process of how life works, so there's always quite a number of them. They are not about to be in a meeting like this and are better off being in a meeting that teaches "how Humans work". Many of them wind up on the psychologist's couch to discover more about themselves and, oddly enough, many even end up being psychologists themselves! This is because Human nature is such a vast mystery to be solved by them that they are fully aware how much they need help, so they help other newbies.

LEARNING: Within a few lifetimes, many arrive at a certain state where there is an intuitive awareness of how things work on the planet. There is a better emotional balance and then that Human is a *learner*. Spiritual knowledge can start to be collected.

Learners are an obvious category. These are the ones who are the potential awakeners, for these are the ones who have the potential to come to a place like this, hear the truth, recognize it or not, and leave. If they don't feel it's something they relate to, it just means the timing isn't right. Again, remember the axiom about returning to a less-aware state? You can't. So even if you don't agree with something or act on something today, it doesn't mean you forget it.

Today's foolishness can become tomorrow's wisdom. It just depends on your perception.

Timing is everything. My partner has asked many times, *"Kryon, why did I have to awaken to the truth in the middle of my 40s? It would have been so much more efficient if it had been in my 30s!"* The answer I have given is all about timing. It's about placing him at the age he needs to be in order to do what he does now, and also what he's going to do next. I'll get to that.

And so, dear ones, those who sit in the chairs in front of me and who are reading are all in the *learning* category. These are often the older souls and the ones who have awakened to spiritual questions. They sense what is happening on the planet and want to know more. They have a new awareness that the energy is changing and that the earth needs them. They also know that each path is different, so they are sitting in this room now or reading this transcription with that in mind.

This is the way it works, old soul. Some of you have awakened to the spiritual truth of the "Creator inside" many times. Your library is thick with spiritual purpose. Some of you have just awakened in this lifetime and realized you're an old soul. So since you are all here listening and reading, I'll give you a diversion. It's a complexity you didn't expect and one for the new energy.

An Advanced Complex Quantum Attribute

This may be complex, but some of you are ready for it. This idea is intuitive to some here, for it's spiritual logic. I mention this only briefly, since I have given it before and it needs to be included to make the *winds* explanation as complete as possible.

As I have told you, inside of you there is a library of the Akash. That is to say that there is a truth that you can pull from that is universal. But in a very linear way, you also understand that you can only have in your Akashic library what you have gleaned from your lives on Earth. True or false? We have spoken of this before in this new year of 2013. The answer is, it depends on how quantum you become.

Now, this is very difficult, but now I broach a subject that is completely nonlinear, so listen carefully. If it is true, dear Human Being, that you were seeded by an ascended race from another part of the galaxy [The Pleiadians], that means that you have a piece of their DNA! Everything that they know is in your DNA – and you know where I'm going with this, don't you? That means that you can awaken to great amounts of truth, but truth that is not based on Earth experience. Instead, it's there from what they gave you. This goes way beyond what we have taught you about your Akash, and takes it into a *spiritual quantum Akash*.

There will be some who ask, *"Well, then, we come in with that, right? Even the newbie has that? So why don't we remember it?"* The answer is this: In the new energy [past 2013], there will be those who will start to use what we will call "quantum Akashic tools". Included in these will be the idea of "mining the Akash" [an attribute we have given before] and also the idea of "quantum Akashic inheritance", which will be the beginning of remembering *original galactic ancestor knowledge*. This will eventually lead to quantum invention on the planet. As Humans become more quantum in their evolution, they will start to pick up these new tools. It's DNA related, and we have spoken of it many times. It's "remembering". But these things will only begin happening to the oldest souls among you, for it happens only after full realization of "God inside".

Karma

How does karma play into all this? The learner, who is the one who gets past the state of just "arriving on Earth", now has something called karma, and it's a big energy to work with. So let's explain what it is.

Karma is "unfinished family group energy" that continues from one lifetime to another. It pushes and pulls you around life, and it has nothing to do with predestination. Instead, it has everything to do with *predisposition*. If you have a lot of karmic energy around you, then you are predisposed to move left or right when certain conditions happen. This is based upon the energies of the past and comes mostly from Human interaction.

We gave you information back in 1993 when Kryon Book One, *The End Times*, was published. We told you that old souls now have permission to drop the energy of karma and steer their own way through life, co-creating the energy of what they want instead of having to battle the past. We continue to tell you that karma is an old system of learning and you are now beyond it.

Karmic energy is still needed for the learners who are not ready to drop it and who need to walk through lessons based upon it. Karma is not available to the newbie [first-timer], since the new soul coming in has no past energy to pull from. By the way, that's why they are clueless! But by the second or third time around, they start creating their own karma from the energy of ordinary life that then pushes them to do things in the next life.

Once the old soul has dropped karma, it means that he has severed it completely and the next time around, it won't be there either. Again, here is a quantum attribute that states that, "what you create within the patterning of your spiritual DNA today stays forever. It does not have to be done again in the next life." Again, this is not predestination, but know that what you do in this life shapes the next, and in this new energy it is profound, old soul!

Contracts – A Reveiw

I want to talk to you about *contracts*. The very word is misunderstood. Do you feel you have a spiritual contract to *do something* on Earth? Some of you will arrive on the planet and will think, *"I am here doing what I'm supposed to be doing in this city because it is my contract."* So while you are seemingly fulfilling your contract, what do you do when another person comes along with a better offer, but you have to move to another city? It might be a spiritual offer, placing you in a far better place to help people. Oh no! Here is a big puzzle. What happens with your spiritual contract?

Part of you pulls in the direction of, *"I must stay here and do what I came for."* The other part of you is torn with indecision. Finally, you bolster yourself and say, *"My contract is that I must stay here and do my work. No matter what, I will fulfill my contract with God."*

Let me give you a word to remember – nonsense! Your contract is in invisible ink! Listen, old soul: Every single day of your life has a rewritable spiritual path. Did you know that? This is the essence of co-creation. The only contract you have is to *be here*, and it is being fulfilled as you read this. So pick up the spiritual pen and write what you need every day. If synchronicity comes along and sweeps you into another area, view it for what it is – it's what you asked for! Feel the truth of it as it occurs. Go with your intuitive feeling and write a new contract for today, which can disappear tomorrow as you rewrite it into something even better.

Old soul, you've never had an opportunity like this before. In this new energy you can change the Wind of Existence to match what you need. In these next few years, you'll decide a number of things collectively on this planet. Through very slow attrition of the old energy dying out, you will gain the upper hand.

There will be greater integrity, and old souls will create it. Sometimes the old souls will be represented in young bodies that are awakening quickly. The very plan of what the earth is about will start to take shape. New alliances of nations will take place. More borders will drop, and governments will start to understand a new principle of unity that has never been seen before on the planet. It will eventually create the seeds for real peace on Earth. Even the Middle East will shift.

I've said it before: There will be future generations who will look back and identify everything before 2012 as, *"The Barbaric Era"*. You will see civilization as you know it start in 2013. That is the promise of a real demarcation point coming within three generations. Think about it. Human history has always been about war and conquering; however, you are beginning to turn a corner. As the old energy slowly dies away, survival will be seen as unity and cooperation. It's already happening on the planet, did you notice?

The Wind of Existence is you, working the puzzle, old soul, and you're not in karma and you're not in a contract. Instead, you're in *manifestation mode*. It may not seem like it, but give it a chance. We've said this before: When you start getting out of survival mode and stop worrying about every single thing, you eventually arrive at manifestation mode. The *worry mode* is what your parents were taught. You inherited it, but it's not what enlightened beings do. Instead, they manifest what they need and they don't worry about what they don't have, for it comes to them when they need it through the process of synchronicity – an enlightened concept that gives credibility to the divine wisdom inside.

The Wind of Transition

The last wind is the Wind of Transition. You call it death. What can I tell you about this that you don't already know? Well, I think I can tell you a lot. First of all, the rules: You don't know what you don't know. You don't know when it's going to happen. Did you know that we need to keep some of you here for a very long time? It's because you are not done with what you started. For others of you, we need you to transition sooner rather than later in order to follow your own plan. We need you at a new place on the planet soon when you're young. We need your Akashic knowledge to awaken early and keep developing what you're developing now, because you have the energy of youth.

We need you to be a certain age so you can run for office, just as you planned. We need to have you young for other reasons that should be very obvious to you as you think about it from our standpoint. So, you don't know when you are leaving. Cast away the fear of this transition, so you understand the reasons that are profound and the ones you helped create when you were on my side. The very awakening process helps to decide when you're going to transfer the energy and move through transition yet again.

I want to give you an attribute you probably haven't thought of: Death is fearful. In the corporeal sense, you have an incredible will to survive. The last thing anyone wants, even bacteria, is to die. Survival then pushes you to live and nobody simply walks into death without fear. This will remain, and it's the way it should be. But there is a gift that we give you, and you don't even know about it.

At the moment of transition, when your heart stops and you take your last breath, we are there. All the angels from the Great Central Sun are there, too, and they kindle a light that puts you at peace. It's a peace so great that fear cannot exist. In a fraction of a second, you know it's OK. You might call it a *spiritual anesthetic*, but we call it "the gift from the Creator."

So the Wind of Transition from our standpoint, a quantum standpoint, is beautiful. It represents that instant where you realize you're finished with this life. It's only for a second, and then it's gone. Then you move into the process of a three-day remembrance of who you are. Part of you is still on the planet and part of you is with us. All of it is beautiful.

Some Humans have gone through a near-death experience and explained it the best they could, but they all say they came back different. Oh, Human Being, they saw a piece of it; they saw a piece of the creator and when they came back, they exclaimed to you, *"You won't believe it! I was dead for a moment and I heard singing and saw light."* Just ask them and they'll tell you. So this is the gift of transition that we have never talked about before. There is no sting in death, Human Being. The only sting is for the ones who remain and don't know where you are. They feel you are gone forever, but you are not. Neither are the souls of those you have lost over the years, dear listener and reader. Did you know that the parents you may have lost will be with you till your last breath? They are holding your hand the whole time. This is complex, but it's part of a beautiful, multi-dimensional system of soul grouping. Some of you know I'm right, since you have sensed them.

Human Beings, you have to know that your soul group can be in several places at the same time. We've given you that information before. Souls can be reincarnated somewhere else on the planet as a corporeal Human, and also be with you at the same time as what you perceive as a guide. Don't ask the question about "how", because it won't make any sense in your reality. It's a beautiful system. Death has no sting!

If you lose somebody you love, I want you to remember this: They may appear still and cold and gone forever, but that's just in 3D and it's not the truth. They are alive and well and looking at you, pleading with you to see the energy of love that they represent. They are not gone.

Those are the Three Winds for today. I love to talk about these things, for they are near to me all the time. I work with all three, and I'm working with them right now. The energy that is Kryon is a group. It's just like all of you are, since you also have these attributes. I'm part of a group right now who are working with those at the Wind of Birth. I am also welcoming those going through the transition – right now. This is the role of Spirit through the Higher-Self that is yours. Discover God inside. When you do, you will also see that the plan is beautiful, dear ones.

And so it is.

Kryon

Final Thoughts
Kryon Book 13
by Lee Carroll

I was looking back over the book and was thinking about writing some kind of summary. Then I hear the sweet voice of Kryon saying, *"It's not finished yet."* I laughed. Kryon is right. For 23 years, each book led to another and then another. Now others are even compiling my Kryon information into other books. Yes, it will continue for a long time, perhaps even when I'm gone.

This book felt different. There was a sense of urgency and celebration from Kryon all at the same time. I have pondered this for awhile. Why does Kryon want to dwell on new balances of dark and light, and all that information on the Crystalline Grid? As an author, I wondered if it was too redundant. But as a channeller, I know that repetition is needed for new listeners and readers. But this book was different. It's also smaller than some in the past. I wondered about adding more channellings, but the subject seemed complete.

I'm now realizing that I'm actually feeling "the compassionate energies of Spirit". Indeed, it is urgent! There have been subtle messages from Kryon that this galaxy has experienced this before. This event is not new to them, but it is to us. Passing this time marker and going beyond the millennium shift and on past 2012, was not in the cards when I was born. Now we all sit here in this energy and many of us can feel how different it is.

So I went into my channelling mode (no, my head doesn't spin around), and decided to write down what Kryon wants to say to finish this book. It's on the facing page.

Thanks again for your support of the Kryon work!

Lee Carroll

Greetings dear ones, I am Kryon of Magnetic Service.

Kryon - what am I feeling that is different right now? Is there something you wish to say to the readers of this book?

Many of you have children. You watch and protect them because you are wise in life. You know how children are, and know in advance how the stages of growth will be. Still, they have free choice to do whatever they wish with their thoughts and later on, their actions as adults. What do you wish for them? How do you feel when they are graduating from their schools, or standing on stage, singing with other children? Your heart is in your throat.

You have been through this as adults, so you know what is next for the young ones. But they do not. They think they do, but they don't. With each victory, comes a new chance to grow further.

I have seen this graduation of consciousness many times over the past eons of time within this galaxy. There is nothing to prepare you for the grandness of an entire consciousness shift. Why so much talk about dark and light? Because you have been "trained" to misunderstand it, and now you need to understand the truth. A lower consciousness carries child-like attitudes, traditions, and beliefs. Now it all starts to focus into common sense and spiritual logic.

We stand back and weep with joy at the event, and at the same time we have the anticipation and expectations before us of what we have seen with the other planets in the past. This is a magic time for you, old soul. When I see you next, on my side of the veil, you will be so anxious to "get back and finish the job!" I've seen it before.

Never has there been a grander spiritual awakening on the planet than this. The potentials are immense! Too slow for you? Patience! You are right on schedule. And so it is!

www.kryon.com

Free Audio online!

No subscriptions • No passwords
No disclosing personal information
No fuss • No e-mails needed
... just FREE

[www.kryon.com/freeaudio]

Check out the many channellings and even some former Kryon audio books and discontinued audio CDs at the above Internet address. Download these free MP3 files and put them in your iPod or just listen on your computer. These are full stereo, high-quality live recordings of some of the most profound Kryon channellings in an updated and growing library.... hundreds of hours!

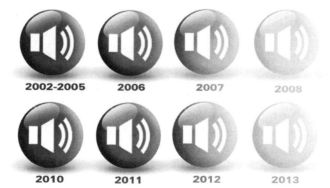

2002-2005   2006   2007   2008

2010   2011   2012   2013

First Ever
Kryon-Compilation Book!

Representing the channellings of KRYON through Lee Carroll.

TITLE: **The Gaia Effect**
The remarkable system of collaboration between Gaia and Humanity

AUTHOR: **Monika Muranyi**

[**www.monikamuranyi.com**]

ISBN: **978-2-896261-132-1**
Price: **16.00 $US**
Publisher: **Editions-Ariane**

Available on the KRYON STORE
[www.kryon.com/store]

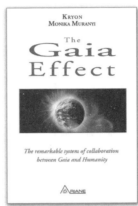

Have you ever wondered about Earth energies, ley lines, portals, sacred sites, hauntings and more? If so, than this is definitely the book for you. Australian author and naturalist, Monika Muranyi, has compiled everything that Kryon has ever channelled about Gaia!

For over 23 years the loving messages of Kryon, as given by Lee Carroll (the original Kryon channel) have become known world-wide. This book represents an amazing job of research that covers many topics that have never before been published by Kryon. Monika's personal experiences and insights weave together the Kryon teachings and wisdom to present a very unique picture of our origins and why we are here.

In addition, she has posed over thirty new questions answered by Kryon. Thanks to her work we now have greater understandings about Earth energies and how these interface with humanity in this first-time-ever compilation of Kryon material.

Drop by and visit
KRYON CENTRAL

The award winning Kryon website allows you to find the latest information on seminars schedules, and Kryon related products. Browse through portions of Kryon books, read some of the most profound Kryon channellings, enjoy some of the hundreds of answers in the Kryon Q&A section, and watch free videos.

Kryon's website offers the latest in technology and is easy to navigate. Our main menu allows you a very simple guide to all the main areas of our site. It is formatted specifically for mobile devices too!

 STORE

 Q&A

 SEMINARS

 GET CONNECTED

 VIDEO

 FREE AUDIO

CONTACT

CHANNELLING

www.kryon.com

What is this thing?

From Lee Carroll

To those in generations before computers and lasers, this was known as a "caliper". Calipers are still around, but in every day life, we don't see them often. So the metaphor, of course, is that we are recalibrating everything around us, but especially ourselves.

The Human is in the bubble, being measured between the caliper's arms. This metaphor is humanity recalibrating. However, I created two things that are subtle: (1) The bubble is the Merkabah, that multi-dimensional field that Kryon says we all have. (2) The Human figure is... well... take a look. Is He/she wearing a dress? Ha! Sure is! I did this to represent all the women who only see standard male icons everywhere (except bathroom designators). It's a standard and I just broke it! So the figure represents both genders, since the top half is the standard masculine, and the dress is the feminine side. It's a balance! Maybe this icon will catch on?

Lee Carroll

A PROFOUND DNA ACTIVATION PROCESS
by Jan Tober

JAN TOBER is an International speaker, healer, and facilitator.
She is co-author of the best selling Indigo Children series Hay House books, having introduced the very term "Indigo Children" to the public along with Lee Carroll, in 1999. Co-creator of the Kryon work, she travels with Lee internationally, bringing her healing voice to thousands.

In recent years, Jan has been able to offer her unique personalized DNA sound activation process, and the international reviews are unanimous and inspiring. Using the crystal bowls from CRYSTAL TONES [**www.crystalsingingbowls.com**], Jan creates a custom CD recording, guided by gathering your personal birth information. This is a DNA activation and ascension process that she has developed over many years, using her healing voice and the renowned quality of the singing crystal bowls... even a special KRYON BOWL!

Please visit Jan's website for ordering and price information: [**www.jantober.com**]

UP CLOSE
WITH KRYON!

Get together for a personal afternoon or evening with Kryon and Lee Carroll in the comfort of a community center or intimate hotel conference venue with a small group of dedicated Lightworkers. It's the most popular way to join in the Kryon energy in the USA and Canada.

The special meeting starts with an introduction and discussion by Lee Carroll regarding timely New Age topics, then it continues during the day with profound, inspired teachings from the Kryon work. It finishes with a live Kryon channelling. Group size is typically 75 to 150 people. Often lasting up to five and a half hours, it's an event you won't forget!

To sponsor an event like this, please contact the Kryon office: e-mail <kryonmeet@kryon.com>. For a list of upcoming event locations, please see our Website page [www.kryon.com/events].

Kryon at the United Nations

Lee Carroll - UN visit 2005

Seven times since 1995, Lee Carroll and Kryon have been invited to lecture and channell at the S.E.A.T. (Society for Enlightenment and Transformation) at the United Nations in New York City. By invitation, he has brought a time of lecture, meditation and channelling to an elite group of U.N. delegates and guests.

Kryon Book Six, Partnering with God, carried the first two entire transcripts of what Kryon had to say... some of which has now been validated by the scientific community. Kryon Book Seven, Letters from Home, carries the meeting in 1998. The 2005 and 2006 transcriptions are in Kryon Book Eleven, Lifting the Veil. All Seven of these transcripts are on the Kryon Website [www.kryon.com/channelling], up through 2009.

Our sincere thanks to Zehra Boccia for her help with introducing us to the presidents of this organization over the years. We thank the S.E.A.T for the invitations, and for their spiritual work, which helps to further enlighten our planet.

Index

Africa.. 129

Akash............45, 46, 116-117, 129, 143
.... 145, 187, 212-228235, 234, 245

Akashic drivers 216, 225

Akashic Inheritance 44-45, 84
...........................116-117, 209, 221, 245

Akashic readers 238

Akashic wisdom.......................... 129

Alignment timing........................... 21

Ancient prophecy...............13, 26-30

Anger......................................189, 194

Animals reincarnation (pets) 141

Artists..237

Atlantis Syndrome 222

Big picture.................................... 85

Biology calibration...............42, 100

Biology not from Earth 234

Black hole (center of galaxy) 89

Braden, Gregg 14

Bridge of Swords 58

Broadcast news 133

Changing – children....................101

Changing the past 88

Channelling experience 76-80

Chilam Balam...............................17

Children – changing....................101

Clearing the past......................... 46

Cold fusion 63

Common cold 48

Communal living..........................114

Consciousness shift.............. 89, 96

Conspiracies................................181

Constant bias................................. 11

Contracts (spiritual).....177-178-179
.... 246-248

Cooperative energies 47

Dark and Light................ 58, 94-109
.... 162-166, 169, 177

Dark entities 95, 164, 170-174

Dizziness 43

DNA 43, 50, 64-72, 78-79
87, 101, 118, 125, 134, 141-150, 216-224
.... 234,245, 257

Don Alejandro...............................27

Drama 127

Eagle and the Condor 26

Earth polar flip............................. 10

Economy..106

Ego...188, 194

Electricity (energy).51, 62, 130, 202

Elijah......................................144, 149

End of war 135

Energy (electricity).51, 62, 130, 202

Energy (general) 155

Entanglement............................. 143

Evil.............. 58, 95, 162, 169, 171, 174

Fear........... 46, 152, 162-165, 170, 175
.... 188, 193, 217

Financial – shift.......................... 105

Food (advice) 115

Fractal time 14

Free will 51, 125, 154, 215

Index

Fresh Water 130

Fusion – cold............................. 63

Future timing 51

Gaia 141-150

Galactic alignment 19

Geoff Stray 23

Global Coherence Initiative.......... 31

Global Consciousness Project..... 31

Governments 42, 51, 93, 103-104

.....................................125, 204. 248

Gregg Braden 14

Hemisphere balance..................... 41

Higher-Self 110, 125, 143, 145

.... 171, 200-201, 232-235, 251

Human quantum field 145

Human soul 231

Human spiritual system 236

Index (you are reading it) 260

Innate 44, 142, 145, 102, 116-121

.... 216, 174, 193, 216, 225

Integrity 131

Intelligent design 85

Invention 41, 53, 57, 73, 108

.... 119, 132, 184, 202, 245

Jaguar priest...............................17

Jorge Bianchi............................. 149

Jorge Baez.................................. 14

Journey – Feathered Serpent......25

Judgment 190, 196

Karma 245

Kinesiology 145

Kryon – UN quote.........................25

Kryon Gaia – book........................33

Kryonites.....................................3

Kundalini 26, 41, 96

Left Behind – book 11

Lemuria............. 55, 62-65, 71-74, 118

.... 223-225

Light and Dark............... 58, 94-109

.... 162-166, 169, 177

Longer life 128

Lost information......................... 14

Magnetics – Solar System.......... 86

Master numbers 32

Masters (Spiritual).................... 149

Mayan calendar 15-22

Medicine (advice)........................118

Merkabah.......144, 150, 202, 221, 256

Monika Muranyi........................... 34

New physics................................ 62

New Pope 127

News broadcast 133

Nibiru 11

Nikola Tesla 62

North Korea 135

Nostradamus 9

Old energy................................. 60

Old Soul 160, 242

Parking Angel.............................. 61

Past lives (akash discussion) ... 221

Physics – new............................ 62

Physics (conversation)..........63-74

Pleiadians......30, 65, 72-74, 118, 229
.... 245, 201-202
Politics 104, 133, 207
Pope (New) 127
Precession equinoxes . 15, 18-21, 198
Prediction (general) 107, 127, 134
Predictions – science 73, 90-91
Proof of compassion 31
Quantum factor 52
Quantum field (Human) 145
Reincarnation of animals (pets)
.... 141, 235
Rewriting history 20
Science – predictions 73, 90-91
Seed inheritance.......................... 128
Seeding of the planet................. 201
Self-worth................. 49-50, 159, 161
.... 172, 176, 183, 220, 224-225, 237
Shift – financial 105
Sid Wolf – dedication.....................3
Solar System magnetics............. 86
South America............................. 136
Spiritual contracts 178-
Spiritual Masters........................ 149
Spiritual systems (change)....... 126
Spontaneous remission 150
Steve Jobs – dedication.................3
Ted Noel.. 12
Temple of Rejuvenation 64, 70
The Crystalline Grid.......30, 100, 137
.... 146-148, 156-159, 172, 200-210
The Dark Rift 21

The Gaia Effect.............................33
Thirty three (33) miners.............. 21
Tim Lahaye 12
Time 83
Timing – future 51
Todd Ovokaitys, M.D.................... 62
Tradition 121
Twenty twelve (2012) energies.. 40
Uncomfortable biology 43, 50
Universal recalibration 82
War (end of)................................. 135
Water (fresh).............................. 130
Weather.. 61
Wind of Birth...............................233
Wind of existence....................... 241
Wind of transition..................... 248
Woody Vaspra...............................25
Worship 113
Xochicalco Mexico 15
Yawee (conversation with) ... 63-74
Zecharia Sitchin 11